TO MAKE A LIFE

Daniel Walser

Cover by Brandi Murphy

For information:
www.tomakealife.com

ISBN 978-0-9859037-0-1

For Julia

TABLE OF CONTENTS:

- PROLOGUE -

My first attempt at words after it happened was like drawing blood with a screwdriver. It was slow, messy, agonizing work. Muscles, mind, and soul straining. I look at the journal page now, and still see that these are not normal letters. They are a battered alphabet, hunched over and crooked, lines of oppressed slaves seeking shelter - anything but the scorching heat of the page, anything but being forced to labor alongside one another to make manifest what feels like unspeakable horror, like the blackest shadows of humanity, like the absence of God. My entry reads:

All our stories seem to begin and end with sorrow. Deep, penetrating, helpless despair that vices tighter and tighter around your throat, choking the faith out of you forever. I have proof now that I am but a splintered marionette commanded by a cruel puppeteer to act out a tragedy, not a comedy. No laughing at a wedding, no dancing at a festival. In the climax of our play, the whole of the cast is mourning. The sun has been stolen from me. When will there be a break in the shroud?

And what of God's silence? Never has faith seemed so unreasonable, even ridiculous, and yet so necessary, even life-giving. Am I to trust that a loving Being joins me in this suffering? Am I to trust that some compassionate Presence is with me, walking each bloody step over broken glass scattered on the path of my broken dreams? Promise after promise in the Bible reads: "I am with you." Shouldn't this be the day where faith is no longer required? Shouldn't this be the exception; that as I fall to my knees and weep for my dead child, the hand of God must physically press on my shoulder? Why, in the midst of this profound misery, should I also have to muster up the fantasy, the imagination, that Christ is comforting me? I ask God this - no answer. Job said to Him, "You dissolve me in a storm." And this is what grief feels like: The lightning crashes just long enough to see yourself disappearing.

Our journey is garnished with unique experiences, singular twists and turns that we've navigated, particular scenes we've played a role in, but in truth, our narrative is no different than yours, than any human being's on this earth. You too were given breath out of your mother's womb. Your eyes were opened on a world teeming with wonder, with breadth, with possibilities unnumbered. You grew. You witnessed. And what did you see? What did you feel? Whether you were thirteen or thirty-three, and whether you articulated it or not, you felt at some marked moment the piercing pain of being cut by a shattered cosmos. A tear in the fabric of your soul. A cannon shot that propels you to a place where for the first time, you feel the mileage between yourself and your God. And it's always paired with a paralyzing fear that you are all alone. So these shoddy, uneven thoughts in my journal might be your thoughts, these heavy questions might be your questions, or perhaps yours are a different shape, a different color, a different sound. But we all know the rumble of that distinctly human cry rising from our depths, the core lament of a created being wailing out in the middle of a storm begging He that commands the winds and the waves to make it stop.

I want to invite you into my storms and my confrontations with the God who claims, "Come to me, all of you who are weary and carry heavy burdens, and I will give you rest." My prayer is that we might stumble together, heal together, and find hope together. We who often grapple around in the dark trying to make a life on this ever-mysterious planet, may we see that God is, even now as you read these words, the light that will never fade, never falter, and will always lead us to the greatest treasure on earth: Himself.

CHAPTER ONE

- DREAMING -

"When we are dreaming alone it is only a dream. When we are dreaming with others, it is the beginning of reality."

- Helder Camara

It started with a conversation in a car outside of a grocery store on a Tuesday night. Fall was unwilling to withdraw from Summer, so we took advantage of the warm evening, letting our windows down. Julia shifted slightly, leaning a forearm against the wheel, brushed aside strands of curly blonde hair that had tumbled over her blue eyes, and casually tossed out a what-if that set in motion a shared dream. A dream that has in so many ways shaped the rest of our lives together.

"What if we had a baby?" She said it and I received it with the utmost innocence. Maybe call it ignorance.

Maybe naiveté. What's certain is that this specific exchange of words has gained gravity the longer it rents a room in my memory. But really, it was just this effortless question followed by an effortless conclusion - yes, we can. Concerns were easily dismissed and worries laughed away, fears falling at the feet of that great giant named the bright future. The what-if had become the possibility, the possibility gave way to the dream. Then wide smiles traced with anticipation, a kiss of celebration, and Julia and I exclaiming together: "We're gonna have a baby!"

For Julia, this was a what-if 24 years in the making. Granted, this precise dream was hatched in our car, but the operative word was the "we". The "having a baby" part was already a foregone conclusion for her; it had been simply up to God with whom it would be. Motherhood was an aspiration stitched into every fiber of Julia's being, a desire coursing through her every vein. To characterize it as some carefree daydream would be to weaken it, wobble the legs beneath it, to diminish its solidity, its colossal readiness to come into being. And why shouldn't it be assured? If ever there was a woman born to be a mother, it is my wife. Julia was one of those little girls you'd have to hide your laughter from, only because she is so obviously serious about her reputation as a five-year old mom. I gather even her Barbies accused her of hovering a bit too often, admonishing too strictly over manners at the daily tea party. No doubt her younger sister remembers that life was not always easy when you have two caretakers, one tall and one miniature, with equal passion and diligence for upholding moral codes. But this is not why I believe she was born to be a mother. I believe it because her heart, by its very nature, is perpetually available, already given over to the next person who might need her nurturing. This overwhelming sense of compassion willed her to tuck in each Cabbage Patch kid with tenderness every night. To sustain a stuffed animal through an illness only she could make up and only she could cure. To take her hurting sister's rising temperature and place a cool towel on her forehead. It should be no surprise, then, that Julia grew tall, graduated college with a degree in Nursing, and has since worked on a maternity unit, caring for her two favorites: mothers and babies. So I imagine Julia felt a brand new sensation that night in the car - her soul fluttering open as the present finally seemed to marry her divine destiny. It was peace unhindered. The warmth of God smiling at his child finding a foreknown path, one that would lead to her ultimate joy.

My heritage of parenting propensities was far less inspiring. However, I did love the idea of being a young father. Because a young father is a titan to his children. Memory lane lays down behind me - I detour past teenage damages and middle school messes to that sweet spot where the slide show clicking through my mind abandons the sharp images of actuality and embraces the scattered light and softened detail of the idyllic days before age ten: I am collapsed on the grass in a vast park with my dad and older brother. How did we get here?

We took The Adventure Way, of course. I watch his every move, my father who created this epic journey; he fills the whole frame of my child's lens. And I want to yell out to the kids in passing families, "Can your father run faster than you can ride a bike? Can he haul those bikes with his bare hands over a 20-foot fence? Can he lead you on a trek across miles of green fields, up a hill as high as the Rockies? Can he send you screaming down the other side of that hill, narrowly escaping menacing oaks as he plummets with you toward certain doom? Can he return you home in one piece, help you cheat death time after time? My father can." Too late, a football game has kicked off. My brother and I cling like giggling monkeys to my dad's legs as he rumbles for another touchdown. I wonder if there is a man on this earth that could possibly tackle him. We get up, we get determined, we get so we'd rather die than disappoint him. He is the hero of our fables; so strong, so youthful, so invincible. And we love him. Love him in a way we all wished we deserved - without sight, without suspicion, without sentencing.

So to be a young father, to be a giant, to be a William Wallace, to love completely and receive it back ten-fold, this felt like returning to a home I never wanted to leave. However, if I'm honest, to say that my life-long dream was coming to fruition here in this car would be a lie. I don't think I would have agreed that having a baby can qualify as a dream. How can something so natural, so ordinarily human, so pre-determined, be a dream? Dreams, to me, were always somewhat unreachable. They were future prizes contingent on your willingness to struggle, sacrifice, and persevere for them. Not a couple doing what they already assumed was in the cards: being fruitful and multiplying.

This confidence, this certainty that things were going to play out exactly as we bargained for, was the air Julia and I breathed. Expectations of expected outcomes. And there seemed no ill effects, just constant and consistent affirmation. Not a bad thing, just a true thing. A brief biography of our success: We met on the very first day of college. We fell in love recklessly, hearts exploding on contact. A romance that felt literary - witty introductions and eyes sneaking extra glances like theft made legal and hands touching accidentally on purpose and laughter that proves your living and conflict you're convinced is earth-shattering and kisses that alter history and hugs that warm like Christmas Eve cider and promises that conquer past mistakes and happily ever after that feels ever more like happily her and I. Married on a perfect day with a perfect Hawaiian sunset descending on a perfectly blue ocean. Family and friends wonder if we're too young, we wonder if we're too young, then we all laugh and eat and dance and wipe away joy-filled tears together and no one cares how old we are because life is too short to be concerned when love wins the day. Before I even graduate, I get a job teaching at a college prep school even though I've never taken a single Education course and I just want my wife to eat food daily so her six-foot-seven father doesn't drive down from his blue collar town and blow off my knee cap with one of his dozen shotguns. I'm teaching English - the school is amazing and the teachers are brilliant and the students are more inspiring than I ever could have expected. Paychecks are coming in, and I want to fax a photocopy to my father-in-law. Julia graduates. She immediately gets hired as a nurse at one of the most prestigious hospitals in Southern California. She immediately excels, is immediately beloved, and is immediately fulfilled in serving and rejoicing with new parents bringing new life into the world. Her paychecks start coming in. I don't want to fax mine to her father anymore. We are 24 years old with pockets bulging, especially compared to when I worked at Red Robin and had to wear jeans from Wal-Mart for my uniform that I think were made for a shorter and wider person because they made my crotch look like it started at my belly button and didn't stop until my mid-thigh. We are youthful and vibrant, renting our first place, taking our first trips, reaching our first goals. All this success at the outset, all these expectations met, all this ease, felt like blessing. In fact, if I had a title for God in those days other than God, it would be 'The Great Blesser.' He had met me in the fractured places of my past, mended them, gave me the most beautiful woman on the planet for a wife, then everything else I cared about. So that's why having a baby wasn't a dream. It was just next in line. The new phase in our predictable future. Because when blessings come readily, come plentifully, you don't dream for more blessings, you do the more logical thing - you plan for them.

Our dream was guaranteed, so we kicked opened the stalls and let it roam free. Julia decked it out with all the trappings and twinkling ornamentation of the girlhood fancies she carried like little trophies into marriage. She had names ready. She also had vetoes prepared for mine. In the theatre of her mind, she watched us decorating the baby's room, painting the walls, assembling the crib, planting a pack of stuffed animals inside it, hanging whimsical stars she hand-crafted, and so much more. She foresaw a pregnancy without vomiting, without whoa-your-face-is-rounder weight gain, but instead characterized by a glow that radiated from her very fingertips. She saw a speedy delivery, an angelic baby in her arms, and a massive celebration in the waiting room as I slid out like Tom Cruise in Risky Business to shout the sex and that customary "mom and baby are doing great!" announcement from the top of my lungs. Then years and years and years ahead of the dream growing bigger, better, and beyond beautiful.

~

Yes, I was foolish to mistake as routine that which is by definition a miracle, but more foolish for taking a dream and forcing it to be a plan. Prudence would state this is how you make dreams a reality, for a dreamer without a plan is destined to remain only a dreamer. But plans are confined. Their value resides in their actualization mirroring exactly what they were predicted to be. They are the shackling down of wordless urgings of the soul into limited articulations. They strip from dreams their true nature - dreams are awe inspiring; they cannot be contained within words, boxes, or checklists. They are bigger than us; they require a better version of us. They are elusive, and so often end up looking entirely different than we ever imagined them to be. But plans rip them from their lofty heights, restrain them with the chains of circumstantial projections, and leash them to a manufactured path with fences on both sides. Yes, a plan can be infused with the vitality of a dream, but only so much as a lover's poem to his beloved can be infused with what his love really feels like. Hints of the essence still reside, but once paired down on paper, no amount of dramatic readings will actually emulate the core stirring of that poet in the throes of his true love. I wonder what is lost in this exchange. Because dreams are from God, plans are from man, and something is always lost when that which is eternal becomes temporal.

Proverbs says that "a dream fulfilled is a tree of life." A plan will then try to satisfy itself by planting the tree, but does its fruit nourish in the same way? No. Then why does the fruit of a planned tree taste so sweet? I believe it is because we take pleasure in guaranteeing what the flavors will be. In other words, the most valuable attribute of a dream made into a plan is this: It can be controlled. So I sat with Julia on that Autumn night excitedly transforming our new dream into a plan. Did I feel a twinge of loss in this exchange? Not at all. Not yet.

CHAPTER TWO

- WAITING -

"There is no grief like the grief that does not speak."

- Henry Wadsworth Longfellow

First evidence that you are exiting the realm of expecting expected outcomes: time gets fat. Time balloons into an unfriendly, laborious mass. What is it filled with? The weight of waiting. The dream was born. Then six months passed. Then another six months. Then another. No pregnancy. No success. No pre-destined plans realized.

Our life is so short, "like a passing shadow," the Psalmist says. Yet the struggle to have a baby is, like any hardship, a shadow knocking on the door, shoving itself inside, and moving all its crap into your bedroom. It's all so very slow - you wonder if Jesus accidentally sat on God's remote and is letting too many awful scenes in your life play out in slow motion. It is only and always a process. And it charts like polygraph results - swinging high and low and revealing falsehoods along the way.

~

Julia and I had bound down from the mountainside with a child's dauntless idealism, with a vision of babies galore in our mind's eye that was so clear and so complete we could practically wrap our arms around it. But then we tripped, fell, plummeted down to earth, and realized that the oracle who just foresaw all the triumph and prosperity to come turned out to be a liar. The perfect picture of the future framed in our mind's eye was a fake; an impostor piece that's sunset landscape washed away in the lightest rain.

How does it feel to chase after this fading vision of your dream? Imagine your dream is an oasis thousands of miles away, and you are trying to make the journey to that sweet spot, where the water waits clear, cool, and electric blue. Not simply to taste, but to quench the thirst that wakes you up in the middle of the night, the inner-drought that no ordinary water can quell. The liquid of self-prescribed destiny that you are certain will fill and fulfill.

You start your journey to this oasis on a plane, because why wouldn't you take the fastest mode of transportation? You hold the postcard of your destination in your hand, loosely, for how could it be in jeopardy?

But the plane is grounded. High winds. You shuffle off, gripping the image a bit harder. You hop in a car, face an endless stretch of road, then the engine stalls. You secure the postcard deep in your pocket; rip it out every few minutes to make sure it's still there. You get calls from loved ones. "Keep going," they say, "It's right over the horizon." Then onto a bike, but soon enough, you peer down to discover a flattened tire. And you are likewise deflated. The trees whither beside the road, meld into dust, to desert. But good news, optimism renewed, because you've decided to look a little harder, justify and rationalize a little more deliberately, and you see the oasis like a mirage in the distance! But don't tell me it's a mirage. It can't be a mirage. It is real. You sprint because the threat of resigning to an unfulfilled dream is always chasing you, desperate to devour. Your leg breaks. But you limp on, eyes fastened to the water, still believing it's as brilliantly blue as it was in your waking dreams years before. All moisture has departed now, and you are swallowing sandpaper, screaming as the knee on your good leg pops out of place and you crumble like clay. Friends are beside the road, holding signs that say "Don't Give Up!" But they can't step on the road, can't mend your bones, can't give you a drink. They are encouraging, but only like the most sympathetic visitor seated on the freedom-side of the glass is encouraging to a man on death row. And there you remain. Crawling inch by inch to a paradise you're starting to believe you conjured up in the first place. A dream that would be so much easier to dismiss if every breath weren't contaminated by it and yet impossible without it. And who gives us breath? God. So it is he who gave you this dream, right? This is waiting. And waiting. And waiting. The answer is your destination, but the questions are your destiny.

~

Back to the beginning: the first months are annoying. We'd long before swallowed the fizzy toxin of entitlement, and the nuisance of delay was only that, a delay. There was no future disappointment added to the equation; simply an unnecessary hiccup in the plan with a short shelf-life. How many negative pregnancy tests have we tossed in the trash? Your best friend is expecting? Your sister-in-law is having a girl? No matter - our baby will merely be a few months younger. Okay, a few more months younger. It'll be next month for sure. There's no problem here.

I did not pray about it, and I didn't ask Julia if she was praying about it. Prayer was for legitimate concerns, a sick relative or a famine in Africa, not an issue I couldn't, or wouldn't, acknowledge. To put words to a problem is to give it life, to feed it, to ensure confrontation with it. So we disallowed it words, boycotted its shape and sound and substance; but as we attempted to strangle the life out of it with our own self-imposed silence, it slipped loose, independent of model and mold, and multiplied.

What is the easier thing to put words to? Denial. We had more than enough justifications and rationalizations in our repertoire. "It always takes couples several months to get pregnant. That's normal." "The timing is just off." "We're too healthy to have something wrong with us." "Let's just take a vacation. That always works!" Great points. I couldn't agree more. And I think the best thing about denial is that you can always enlist plenty of people to help you with it. Finding people with the courage to classify and characterize your deepest hurts is almost impossible, but everywhere you turn is another supporter of keeping your pain without a title. They are like well-intentioned cheerleaders bellowing out their rehearsed ra-ra-ra's from the sideline to cover the eerie silence surrounding you, the player on the fifty yard line whose leg just broke in three places. Their cheers must mean you're not even hurt, right? Nothing provides stronger scaffolding for your fortress of denial than a group of ready and willing laborers - that is of course until cold, unfeeling reality swoops in and bulldozes all that's been built.

Reality was waiting for us in a doctor's office a year and a half after we started trying. Julia and I were hoping our doctor, a male infertility specialist, would be returning with good news. He seemed like a nice guy, but also maybe one-eighth creeper. I was fidgety, like my bones itched. My gut was battling for the first time the front lines of a darker future, an obscure mountain forming, the brilliant sun of expectations-met retreating behind it. I looked to my left, my right, behind me. “What?” Julia said, her tone sharpened not by impatience but by the wages of her own inner combat. “Everything is a penis,” I whispered. Her nervous eyes scanned the room: coffee mugs with penis handles, a penis putter, a penis race car, even a Leaning Tower of Weiner. Julia and I glanced at each other - okay, probably more like one-third creeper. A synchronized laugh escaped. It was a gift from God. Not rooms full of penises, of course, but the momentary reprieve from the impact of a diagnoses that comes in a room full of penises. A calm before the chaos that does not stay the oncoming storm, but does let you lean in to one another, fear-to-fear, if only for a few seconds.

We walked out of his office carrying the new knowledge that our odds of conceiving naturally had plummeted fifty stories down to that damp, dreary basement where those waiting to win the lotto or get struck by lightning reside. I did not understand how I could be deficient physically. I was healthy. I was an athlete. I played college basketball. I assumed that my sperm would be wearing headbands, rocking six-packs, and running sprints just to stay game-ready. The idea that they were a few, literally retarded soldiers, bumping into walls and one another like drunk sailors in a sea-storm absolutely confounded me.

In the months that followed, two equally potent forces perpetually framed my thoughts: fear and guilt. Fear for a barren future and my wife’s dreams forever deferred. Guilt that it would be my fault, my defect, my hammer pounding the nail into the coffin lid, burying alive her dream to be a mother. I don't mean to say I was haunted by these ideas every waking second, for one can intentionally fill a day with thoughts that do not cut, do not bully, do not maim the heart. One can, in the busyness of a week, line up a nice list of light topics to occupy their inner and outer dialogue, but in the secrecy and stillness of night, when your head lies heavy on the pillow, those thoughts creep out of the cave you've shoved them in, and they devour without remorse.

And I did not pray. I did not ask Julia if she was praying about it. When the solidity of your God is dependent on the gifts he gives you, the moment you do not get what you want, he is weakened, neutralized, lesser. Why, then, ask of him? If Santa Claus did not show up, if there was only bare wooden boards beneath the tree, would you have confidence in sending a letter to the North Pole with a kind request for delivery of the presents he forgot? Perhaps you would. Not me, though. It seemed far more logical to shake off the betrayal from Santa and go get those gifts myself.

~

I grew up with two parents that loved me and loved one another. We had money and attended a large church. I had good friends who also had two parents, money, and attended a large church. We were, in other's eyes, the epitome of that too often coveted and completely fictitious entity, the functional Christian family. But my 15th year would mark our decline, our American Dream reduced to rubble. The reasons are myriad, but the catalyst was my brother's agonizing courtship with a devastating drug addiction. All who have beheld this know it is a brutal unraveling. The addiction's itchy fingers greedily undo all ties one has to a liberated life so that it might strike and ultimately strangle its prey, the muted victim too enslaved to cry for help.

It was late one school night; I was awake and so were my parents, all of us ingesting the cruel quietude of a house waiting in turmoil for its last wayward inhabitant to safely return. My brother finally stumbled through the door, a prodigal intruder in his own home, his footsteps laden with the latest fix. There was a screaming match in the hall; cursing then crying then the cancerous silence that was too often the crippled lullaby to which I closed my eyes. I woke in the dead of night with a strange inclination to check on him. I slipped unnoticed into his room. He was curled up, a ghostly white fetal ball on a mattress in the corner. Inching closer, I saw that he was sweating profusely, sheets soaked through. He seemed a faulty rocking chair, swaying back and forth with shoulders unglued and joints unhinged. He shivered violently, like some involuntary force was trying desperately to alarm him, to rouse him. I touched his arm - ice stretched over flesh. I recoiled. I watched my brother sweating, and shivering, and suffering, and that's when I decided, "There's no way God can be present in this. No way." The God I knew of was not here - he was in the gigantic church building, filled with all the healthy people. The proof was in the pastors, who had given up on my brother, labeled him a burnout, and so I was convinced that God is not really for the sick and weary and defective, but for those who have their lives together, for those whose families weren't crumbling, for those who weren't waking up in the cold veil of night to find their brother high off his mind, trembling like a neglected newborn left to perish on a winter sidewalk.

That night I met a strain of hurt unlike the others I'd felt. The first cut from a shattered cosmos. The laceration that shrinks your lungs, pours concrete in your stomach, and scribbles one hateful verse on your soul - "We all walk alone." So a dark corner of my heart made room then and there for a new belief, a new mantra. I decided that the best way to live on this lonely planet was for me to take complete control of my life. No God, no others, just me - completely self-reliant. In this way, I might feel occasional letdowns and disappointments, but never again the disarming, destructive pain I experienced that night in my brother's bedroom.

By the time I met Julia at college three years later, I was an eighteen year old kid with a cold heart satisfied with showcasing only a fake, manufactured warm side to the world. But Julia was never impressed nor inspired by my performance. She could, with a look that was both invading yet inviting, set my hands and feet in stone and pickpocket my chilled heart, rifle through its contents, and return them with residual heat from the pure fire of her innocent hands. It was exhilarating. There is a reason I've called her, despite all its cliché connotations, my angel sent from God. For she, through a truly selfless love, introduced me to the God who is love, the God that forgives all sins, the God that can soften what is hardened and make straight what is crooked. Christ for the first time began to transform my callused heart, and I took that initial step into the sunlight of grace granted by his atoning work on the cross.

However, that dark place in my heart, that Need To Control so as to avoid the deepest pains, remained untouched. And Need To Control is a shifty character - he was always content to sit shotgun while God appeared to drive the car of my life, as long as the roads were clear and the ride was smooth. But Need To Control was only biding his time until hardship came - an oncoming truck veering into my lane - because he knows that instantly, I, perched in the back seat pierced with fear and pride, will beg him to snatch the wheel away from God, straighten the path, and save me from danger. In retrospect, the scariest part was not the potential crashes in life, though I would have said so at the time. It was the prospect that as I begged from the backseat, God would lean back, let Need to Control crawl and clutch the wheel, let me think it was he who was straightening the wheels, righting the course, and avoiding disaster without God's help. For is there anything more dangerous than solidifying the belief that He who made the car is less fit to drive it?

~

Yet there I was, more than a year into failing at making a baby, leaning on the door frame of our little bathroom, staring at my wife, my angel sent from God, as she wept bitter, desperate, unyielding tears, her sallow eyes pleading for a second pink line that would not appear. Beseeching a piece of plastic to produce a plus sign that would not even faintly materialize. And my ability to control? Long vanished. I'm in that car, watching the oncoming truck barrel down on us, screaming from the back, and the passenger seat is empty, collecting cobwebs that scoff at me. I am betrayed. Time is wasting, hope is passing away, and the dream is dying. Julia is wearing this reality everyday; a leaden robe that weighs down but does not conceal or protect the one whose back it burdens. And I can't do a single thing about it. It's like I'm back in my brother's room, but the naked fear and emptiness has been infinitely multiplied, because now I'm looking at my wife - crying, and shaking, and suffering; and my heart is being gutted and gouged, and the giant question remains, "God, how can you be present in this?" God who was to me like the Santa Claus that didn't show. I had decided to get the gifts myself. I failed. Consultations and appointments and procedures all for naught - the floor beneath the tree remained empty. Yes, I prayed now, but it was faithless, pessimistic, akin to throwing coins in a wishing well, with the same paltry confidence the castaway must feel as he tosses his message in a bottle into the endless mouth of blue nothingness. Instead I gave root to and steadily cultivated the most destructive offspring of disappointment: self-pity and bitterness. Even worse, I kept them for myself. I knew Julia could be growing her own anger, her own resentment, and yet I would not share it with her. And so we continued to live in that terrible space where denial is ludicrous and acceptance is unthinkable, where you desperately want to share that which you desperately refuse to name.

CHAPTER THREE

- NAMING -

"Love takes off masks that we fear we cannot live without and know we cannot live within."

-James Arthur Baldwin

Silence - that is, the refusal to confess a festering truth - is a merciless overlord, a dictator that reigns over the entire landscape of your most important relationships, forcing you moment by moment to buckle under its subjection, flouting its dominance always. It knows it's strength lies in a deep ideological power that boasts this: Silence has held sway here, in this hardship, for days and months and years, and any attempt at insurrection, a voice of truth and therefore freedom, will only lead to widespread panic, ruin, and swift retaliation. The voice in my head explained it this way: *Dan, you can still handle this. You can't speak of it. Allude to it, fine, but don't dissect it with detail. To admit fully how you hurt, how you've failed to care for her, to accept her distress, only multiplies the harm. It will give her license to resent you. Maybe even hate you. This will be the end of your marriage. Just put your head down - Julia will get pregnant and everything will be fixed. Don't make her share this burden with you. Don't you believe things will get better? Things can always get better.*

But what happens when things don't get better? When optimism has packed its bag and left without a note, and even these 'rational' pleas from Silence ring hollow? I stood in that doorway, watching Julia weep, and I realized for the first time that I was desperately needy, completely out of control - my formula for the fulfillment of our dream had blown up, and the shrapnel was slashing and puncturing and blinding me. What I wanted was a clean slate, a clean conscience, a clean emission that might purge all these fears that mingled with the marrow of my bones. My dad explained once that in the midst of a difficulty like this, in the midpoint of a silent hardship, the beginning of healing only and always begins with one step: Naming it.

I had to give it words. Acknowledge it. Name it. I had to avoid any more half-measured explanations of my feelings. I had to describe each one, inch by inch and corner by corner. I had to detail the dysfunction, chronicle how I had transformed from an upright, confident man to a feeble slave to silence, prostrate on the floor, hands clenched, neck taut. The risk: painting a picture of your heart's greatest discontent before the very person you've been hiding it from. What a gamble to allow all the questions, convictions, and trepidations pour forth from your chest like unruly paint, each a different color but none less vibrant, and splash them on a now visible canvas. The prospect of Julia viewing my heart's painting, my slipshod work of art, in its entirety, scared me more than anything. But I did it.

Julia cried, yes. She withstood the most acute pain, yes. But something extraordinary happened when honesty finally occupied the gaps between us. Her face, though stained with tears of disappointment, did not drop to the floor in defeat. The gloom I had yet to recognize until now was, to my absolute surprise, receding from her gaze. Her eyes had been for months like two birdcages crowded with crows, but now it was as if the wire doors had finally bust open, the ink-black poachers driven out, and the delicate, nearly suffocated blue jays finally given their home back and the liberty to take trembling gulps of untainted air. And so she too began to let her heart gush freely, her colors of worry and of hurt just as vivid as mine, cascading from her chest in a chaotic rainbow of disordered truth. We let it flow together, cupped it in our hands together, and tossed it on the canvas together. Back and forth we went: *I'm so sorry, this is all my fault. No, it's my fault. What if we never have a baby? Do you wish you married someone else so it would be easier? I want to fix this and I can't. God, I'm so pissed I can't fix this.*

You're not really a woman until you have a baby. What kind of man can't get his wife pregnant? I can't do this another month. I'm drowning. I'm drowning and you're just watching. Will this be the end of us? I feel so alone. I can't do this alone. What is God doing? Where is He? Everyone else has babies so easily. I'm jealous. I'm angry. I feel embarrassed, ashamed. I need you to share this with me. I need you to tell me there's hope. I'm so sad. I'm so sad. What do we do? What do we do now?

Our painting was an eyesore, never destined for museum fame. What would seem a hideous mishmash of reckless confessions to anyone else was something measured, meticulous, and meaningful precisely because it was ours - it was shared, it was real, it was true. It was named. This was the beginning of healing. Not surface level alleviation. It was the healing that burns then refines then cools in the hidden spaces of your soul. Healing that turns your face to God. How do we see him? In the forgiving eyes of others. Cramped in that small corner of our home, I confided all this ugliness, and Julia looked on me not with judgment. Not with anger. Only with grace. Not inches of it, either, but miles and miles of grace that covers all. Something profound changed in me that day. All this pent up need for control, this crippling angst and mistrust, was now released, given to God, and for the first time I digested the startling truth that he is most visible where we are most broken. I had constructed a house of morality, of self-help, of self-sufficiency that I planned to pretty up and invite God into. We could share a meal that

I cooked; he would take a few looks around, smile broadly, and exclaim, "Love what you've done with the place." What I understood finally was that God had never actually stepped inside. He was waiting patiently, lovingly, in the decaying and decrepit shack out back where my sins and sadness and shame were packed wall-to-wall like the product of a hoarder's illness. And Christ remained there amidst the cluttered sickness, anticipating my arrival. All these years I assumed my brother was the prodigal. But it was I who was crawling home humbly, humiliated, only to be generously wrapped in the warmth of the father's robe and bolstered by the power of his ring on my finger. And I felt Julia right beside me. Still injured, but not without God. A big difference.

This was the first time I could even comprehend what Paul says in 2nd Corinthians 12. He speaks of a thorn in his flesh that tormented him, left him languid, left him vulnerable. He says, "Three different times I begged the Lord to take it away. Each time he said, 'My grace is all you need. My power works best in weakness.'" It is comforting to know that Paul begged the Lord to make it stop, if only because I have done this so many times myself. It is more comforting, however, to know that when the Lord did not remove it, Paul was confident and blessed to say, "So now I am glad to boast about my weaknesses, so that the power of Christ can work through me. That's why I take pleasure in my weaknesses, and in the insults, hardships, persecutions, and troubles that I suffer for Christ. For when I am weak, then I am strong."

A startling paradox. For so long I had been inhaling weakness, choking on it, then breathing out even fuller desperation, fuller frailty. But now, by the grace of God, though I was drawing in lengthened breaths of that same weakness, I was exhaling strength - a quiet strength that comes from God beside me in that tattered shack out back whispering with cosmic fearlessness: "Let me build you a real home. Then we'll dwell together and share a meal that truly satisfies. And you will turn to Me, and exclaim, 'Love what You've done with the place.'"

And I prayed. With Julia. For Julia. I prayed rightly. I stopped treating God like Santa Claus, and approached him as what he calls himself: a loving and gracious Father. Most gracious in allowing his creation to know completely the scope of his love and the peace that comes from choosing to follow him, that comes from stating with Paul that, "I have been crucified with Christ. It is no longer I who live, but Christ who lives in me. And the life I now live in the flesh I live by faith in the Son of God, who loved me and gave Himself for me."

~

This was not acceptance as it is known in the seven stages of grief. This was something else. Something independent of saying goodbye to the object lost, outside the recognition that a certain dream will never come true. It was a distant cousin to acceptance that's married to contentment and parent to hope. Hope not necessarily for a particular outcome, but hope that comes from a particular source - Jesus. Where there was once a plan, there was now a purpose: "Growing in every way more and more like Christ." Where there was once a dream, there was now the dream: "Seek the Kingdom of God above all else, and he will give you everything you need." But this transformation cannot be trivialized, as though it were similar to starting a new workout routine, quitting smoking, or e-mailing old friends more often. This was, for the first time in our lives, a decision to give everything, even our most precious visions for the future, over to God, a deity whom we'd never physically seen. This was trusting Christ more than ever, knowing that he would provide not necessarily what we want or desire, but "everything we need." So I can never say that deciding to genuinely and wholeheartedly give your life over to Christ is easy. It is anything but, if only because you are immediately smacked in the face with a monstrous truth: Everything. Will. Change. Catastrophic, radically course-altering change in the very make-up of your soul. And as evidence of its authenticity, you will act and do and dare to walk a completely new and often dangerous path. Not necessarily dangerous in that it threatens your life, but dangerous in that it threatens everything else that encloses and informs and insulates your life. It eradicates all barriers between you and Jesus, so that you must lean totally on him. For Christ cannot be a supplement - He is always the whole diet.

CHAPTER FOUR

- CHANGING -

"I do not understand the mystery of grace -- only that it meets us where we are and does not leave us where it found us."

- Anne Lamott

When Julia first mentioned adoption, I immediately had a sour taste in my mouth. Sorry, I thought, I'm not remotely interested in sloppy seconds. I'm not interested in a default dream. Don't you know? God is in control now, and adoption would just be our attempt to regain that control, to complete a counterfeit transaction, a roundabout way to get what we want. Of course in my heart I knew that to be untrue, at least for Julia, because she had been telling me for years that she had a huge desire to adopt. It was I who could not stomach it. Especially now. Maybe much later, after a few of 'our own' kids, we could give it a whirl, but not today, not as a band-aid over the bullet hole inflicted by infertility that was still spouting blood bubbling with disappointment. But as I said, giving Christ your whole heart means you've given him the ability to tame and re-train the wildly selfish ME that howls in the forgotten caverns of your soul, and through his word and his people, he did just that.

The moment I (yet again) relinquished what I thought was right and true, the instant I entertained the idea that perhaps adoption was not a JV dream or a secondary plan, but perhaps God's primary plan, he filled me with a certainty so concrete I nearly toppled over with the extra weight. Everywhere I looked, glimpses of this new vision flashed like little crashes of lightning in my mind, the thunder of God's affirmation resonating down through every bone. Everything we read, conversation we held, video we watched, sermon we sat under, reverberated with the tenor of affirmation; for our destiny as parents, and our destiny as followers of Christ. I was moved by the words in James 1:27 - "Pure and lasting religion in the sight of God our Father means that we must care for orphans and widows in their troubles." And I was convicted by Solomon's plea in Proverbs 24:12 - "Once our eyes are opened, we can't pretend we don't know what to do. God, who weighs our hearts and keeps our souls, knows that we know, and holds us responsible to act." Most of all, though, I was energized by stories of adoption I saw played out by the broader family of Christ. Julia and I watched countless "gotcha" videos that chronicled the homecoming of orphans from all over the world. There's one I know by heart: It starts with pictures.

First a group of Ethiopian women. They are beautiful. One is grinning. One is not. Then a fact - "only 24% of Ethiopian families have access to safe drinking water." Then a gathering of young men on the corner of a busy intersection in Addis Ababa, laughing at other men failing to herd a line of livestock into the road between passing cars. Another fact - "Half the children will never attend school. 88% will never attend secondary school." Then a row of little boys in single file, one in front of the other, each successive face craning a bit further to the side to be seen, like some breezy jazz routine, only in front of a shack instead of an audience. "One in ten children die before their first birthday. One in six children die before their fifth birthday. More than half of those deaths are attributed to malnutrition." Pictures of another family back on our side of the globe. They are praying. They are filling out paperwork. They are posing with posters that showcase their waiting-list number. They are boarding a plane. Then shaky handheld footage of Ethiopia's majestic countryside, a busy thoroughfare, and finally the red gate of an orphanage. A wide shot - scattered strollers and swings and multi-colored toys. Inside - women feeding bottles to new babies, rocking toddlers to sleep, building a tower of blocks with a five year old still waiting for a family. Their sacrificial love for these children is astounding. Back to the shaky camcorder. The mother from across the sea is shaking too; she is about to meet her child. A gracious care-taker hands the squirming infant into her new mother's arms. All are crying and all are overjoyed because though her birth parents, both casualties of HIV, will not be the ones to raise and nurture her, she is no longer destined for hunger, disease, or death. They all clap and sing together. Together. Later, there is an arrival at the airport back home, the reunion, the dozens and dozens of cheering people that will populate the loving community around this gorgeous little girl for years to come.

For Julia and I, to watch this family cry hot, happy tears and celebrate and surround their new addition was breathtaking, and the affection for these children, for our future child, swelled inside us like the purest wave. And this is something that amazes me about God: his ability to take a certain lie that we've chosen to found our lives upon, flip it upside down, and direct us toward an unbridled passion for the exact opposite truth. For me, to adopt an orphan had been to admit defeat and settle for a replacement child. God took that twisted, short-sited, and selfish lie and thwarted it, showered it with his two mightiest weapons, love and truth, and grew it into something wholly antithetical. Now, to adopt an orphan was anything but defeat. It was anything but settling. It was an honor; an invitation to play even the smallest part in God's great design of reconciliation.

~

But in this life, the most crucial choices are always linked with the most crucial speculations. These barricade the new way, halt your course, and interrogate your heart under intense heat lamps. The adoption agency that we partnered with had a very clear rule - you could not pursue having biological children while in the adoption process. There is a host of different reasons behind this, but namely it is to avoid upsetting or upturning birth order, as well as to ensure the adopting couple is in a place physically and mentally to provide the best care for their new child. Reasoning we totally understood. The agency therefore needed a letter from our doctor stating that we were, without a doubt, infertile; that the decision to adopt our first child was made with the acknowledgement that our odds of having biological children were in fact zero. Our doctor wrote the letter. Holding it in our hands and reading the ice-cold explanation dug up that buried pang of a deferred happiness, of hearts once again sore with damaged hope for that damaged dream. But the grace of God abounds - for we believed then and there that to set our eyes solely on Christ was not just the pardon from and surpassing of a despair based on disappointing circumstances, but also, and equally, a license to believe that the impossible was possible, that the dream could still be watered, still nourished, still permitted to grow in the light of the Almighty God, who delights in giving us our heart's purest desires. So yes, we were faced with a decision. But it was not an either-or to me anymore. It was a now-then, a first-second, a blessing followed by a blessing. We decided not to continue to pursue treatments and further medical interventions regarding fertility, but instead be obedient to what God was so clearly asking us to do right now: adopt an orphan.

How odd and how scary is it that to the very end, the life lived for Christ is a constant letting go, a never-ending unloosing of self? And how wonderful it is that as you stand, seemingly alone, eyes sealed shut by fear, hands empty of what you just released, God in turn opens your eyes and shows you palms now filled with that which is infinitely more valuable and infinitely worthier to hold onto. Julia and I decided to adopt our first child from Ethiopia. This calling had been a long, long time in the making - years of the Lord breaking us, re-making us, and guiding us towards obedience. What we had envisioned for our lives on that warm Autumn night in our car was not this - our hearts and minds were chasing other plans and other priorities - none of which pointed to Africa. But slowly, steadily, and surely, God paved the way for his perfect plan. And the result? A quiet peace as the Lord conceived in our hearts a consummate love for the child he would create for our family.

~

The adoption process can be very long and often rife with pitfalls and discouragements. It is costly literally and figuratively. Additionally for us, there loomed the potential of being shoved once again onto the parched path of waiting. However, this interim was altogether different from before. To wait alone is hell. To wait with God is faith. And faith tastes of heaven, a nourishment that never runs dry, even in the most arid wasteland. God was leading us through it all, and we were overjoyed. We were several months, several steps, and several thousand dollars into the adoption process, and I was anxiously awaiting the day when Julia and I could bring our sweet baby home. It was January 12th, 2010 when I wrote this:

I keep seeing my baby's face. When I wake up, as I'm driving to work, just before I fall asleep. The image isn't entirely clear, because I can't even tell if it's a boy or a girl. I can't tell what the eyes, nose, or chin really look like. The only concrete thing I see is an ear-to-ear smile that could light up a city block. One of those smiles that speaks of pure joy, of peace, of being home. And I'm not sure why that's the only thing I can see, but I like it. I like that it's there with me through this maze of paperwork, background checks, and parenting courses. I like that it's present as I'm waiting...and waiting...and possibly waiting some more.

But there's something more - I think my baby's smile shining through the otherwise hazy image in my mind is like our lives, like this whole adoption process. Things get so blurry, so undefined, and it's so difficult to see the big picture. Russell Moore, in his book Adopted for Life, says this: "God often doesn't explain his providence to us, past or future. He asks us to trust him, to endure, and to know, in the words of the old gospel song, that we'll 'understand it by and by.' Sometimes, though, he grants us a glimpse in the middle of it all of how he's silently working toward something joyous.[1]*" I think my baby's smile is that glimpse. And I feel blessed that as we jump over these hurdles, as we wait to see God's perfect timing and his "big picture", He is giving me this glimpse in the middle of it all as assurance that He is silently working toward something profoundly joyous. Because to be honest, I don't think I can even get my mind around the soul-stirring, world-altering gladness I will feel when I finally see my baby's face in all its sweet splendor.*

1 Moore, Russell. *Adopted for Life*. Crossway. 2009.

CHAPTER FIVE

- THANKING -

"Gratitude changes the pangs of memory into a tranquil joy."

- Dietrich Bonhoeffer

Only a few days after I wrote those words, I walked into my bedroom to find Julia crying. I moved closer, concerned; she flicked her eyes up - not dejection, but not elation either - this was a look shaped from being belted breathless, the tears an involuntary outpouring of the body encountering an impossibility. I searched for answers amidst the shock and confusion endorsing her every movement, and found it in the white object lifted from beneath the blankets, the same piece of plastic that had forever only cut like serrated steel, now donning one digital word, bold and unashamed: PREGNANT.

You might assume our first inclination was to jump up and down, pop open some bubbly, dance until our joints failed, and tumble to the floor in each other's arms, screaming delight to the heavens. It was not so. Honestly, the sentiment was closer to the dread two teenagers, after one stupid prom night in the back of a pickup truck, might feel staring at a positive pregnancy test. We were so close to the adoption finish line. So ready to bring our baby home across the Atlantic, to shower it with all the love once bottled up and stifled by infertility, and now it was in jeopardy. We had fallen in love with Ethiopia, with our yet unseen child, with the privilege of being obedient to God's will, with providing rest and peace and promise for an orphan destined for unspeakable difficulties. I saw this on Julia's face. Not eyes that shouted, "What a relief! We're having a baby!" They instead whispered, "What are we going to do now?" Looking back, this amazes me. How God had so molded my wife that though her greatest desire was now coming to fruition, her heart was still anchored to what God had orchestrated and ordained in adoption. I realized that Julia had in fact given her life completely to Christ. That this was never a secondary plan to her - it was a perfect plan. And it hit me; the look she was giving me, the revelation her eyes were offering: this was simply a mother digesting the news that she would have to wait to meet one of her children in the unknown future. This was not motherly love being abandoned, but motherly love reluctantly held for safe keeping.

~

It did not take long for us to unabashedly revel in this miracle - for that is exactly what it was. It was so much bigger than my brain could comprehend. I couldn't believe I was sitting beside my wife, who for so many months had carried the emptiness in her womb like a millstone settled in her abdomen, and now life was growing there instead, life that was light as air and woven with creativity and care and love. Are these not the acts of God that a follower of Christ cherishes more than anything, simply because they seem to undeniably prove his existence? They solidify his unfathomable love. They confirm that he answers prayer. They attest to his faithfulness. And most of all, they showcase the perfect power of a God who exclaims with such zeal, "Therefore I tell you, whatever you ask for in prayer, believe that you have received it, and it will be yours." We had, until this day, only known taxing and disconcerting questions, and in a single instant, the Answer had exploded forth with all the magic and majesty that marks a child's first fireworks show. It was the purest joy! So untainted. So uninhibited. And yes, we did jump up and down. We did dance, as well as two white people can. We did shout praises to the heavens. We sported ear-to-ear grins, giggled like school girls, and fell to our faces in worship. How quickly your knees turn to water and crash to the floor on that hour that God showers you with the very gift you had so often doubted he could give. This is a snapshot I'll always hold onto tightly: Julia's blue eyes wet with tears - brimming with gratitude and emptied of trepidations as she shouted to all who would listen that she was pregnant, that God had heard her prayer, and finally answered.

I was so extremely proud of God. That may sound weird. But I was like the kindergartner with a fireman dad on show-and-tell day, dragging his larger-than-life father to all the other kids who were anxiously waiting to hear his latest tale of life-saving heroism. I wanted to tell everyone that my God is so much more dynamic than Santa Claus. I wanted to shout from the rooftops with Paul, "Oh, the depth of the riches of the wisdom and knowledge of God! How unsearchable his judgments, and his paths beyond tracing out!" I wanted to explain, as it does in Proverbs, that "the heart of man plans his way, but the Lord establishes his steps," and these steps, though they may seem innumerable, and though you may continually collapse on the steep climb, lead to a destination that is incomparably worth the ascent. I was like a boxer who'd been beaten to a pulp for 11 rounds, spitting blood on the canvas and venom at my trainer, whose advice at the end of every drubbing had been simple: "Just wait, the window will open". But with every trip back to the corner, his face had been harder to see, features grotesque and fuzzy. With every round, as I sought his new advice, his new plan, his voice was dimming, deteriorating to the electric hum of a dying appliance. But now! Now in the 12th, as I watched my arm, which had begun to falter like a phantom limb, slice through the air, connect and conquer, everything was crystal. Nothing more so than my trainer's voice, which broke in above the cheers as a bullhorn of celebration and confirmation. And I am reminded that God is not limited, not tied down by science and sin; he is the shaper of destinies that only he can comprehend. For how could we have known that God would take this once busted dream and fashion it into two, each more breathtaking than even the best version of the original? Julia described all of this so well in a blog post for our friends and family:

We will be the first to admit that the road leading up to this came with a lot of heartache. After years of trying to conceive naturally, it was evident that this wasn't God's timing and He had other plans for our future family. While we never gave up on having children biologically, we had resolved to the fact that this wasn't going to happen right now. We had made complete peace with this, and felt God had renewed, restored and changed the vision we once had for our family into a new and beautiful picture that only He could create.

Well this is exactly what He has done. In the last couple of months God has not just blessed us with a deep love for our child across the world, but has seen fit to bless us with a child that will be born to us naturally. Even now as I write, I am still overwhelmed with this news. This was not the plan. Getting pregnant in the middle of our adoption was not the way we thought things would play out. But I tell you this with tears streaming down my face because we are incredibly overjoyed that God has given us these miracles. The miracle only He could have done in leading us to adoption, and the miracle that He has done in this pregnancy. It is obvious that we never knew what this journey would look like, but we are so thankful that God in his sovereignty has known since the beginning of time that this is how our story would unfold.

We are once again humbled. Humbled to be a part of such a story; one that continues to have twists and turns that no one can foresee but our Father. Moving forward, our adoption process will be put on hold until we are allowed to resume the process again. While we might have lost momentary things like time and money, nothing has been wasted in this process and we definitely have not lost our passion for what God has called us to do. We will welcome our first blessing in early October and eagerly await the day we can welcome our second blessing home. God is good, to Him be all the glory.

~

That summer was perhaps the sweetest of our lives. It was a constant procession of little paradises - I found myself grinning at nothing and at everything. Julia and I seemed in a perpetual state of floating, swayed by warm breezes, cool shade, and effortless dreaming about the baby growing strong in Julia's swollen belly. I recognize that I am biased, but trust me, you will not find a pregnant woman more beautiful than my wife. It always caught me unaware - she would simply turn a corner into the room, with one smooth hand resting delicately on the crest of her stomach, and produce a smile so innocent it snatched the breath from my lungs. It was as if God, so overjoyed at what he had created, had caressed for an instant the cheek of our child, and the remnants of his touch were gently diffusing through the rest of Julia's body, magnifying her every movement, kindling her every glance. She wore her happiness like a wedding gown, and her face suffused that rare loveliness that is characterized by eyes emitting unfettered gladness where they once emitted tears.

As confusing, disappointing, and isolating as infertility was, Julia's pregnancy was even more confirming, contenting, and inclusive. All disorientation had finally vanished. That oasis of our dreams had ceased being a mirage; it was clear as crystal, tangible to touch, sure as the sun rising with a new day. And this was a rare and astounding phenomenon: to feel for a time that God was no longer a mystery. To perceive if only for a moment his dimensions, his order, and his symmetry was something akin to sneaking prematurely into heaven's glory, where the veil is lifted, the fog evaporated, and all his truths revealed. I often wonder why God feels much more like a thought than a being, a philosophy than a friend, a figment than a father. But not that summer. In fact, the very absence of having to wonder or guess or question was the refreshment. I am convinced that this is one of the best gifts God can give to a man as he walks on this planet: a reprieve from the illogical nature of unconditional faith. A reunion of the skeptic mind and the optimistic soul. A marriage of the starving earth and the plentitude of eternity. A sweet reconciliation of the seen and the unseen. Time and memory can distort, but even now, I know that this is not embellished nostalgia. Peace had come home to us. And when it did, the house was overrun with those who'd walked with us through infertility, through adoption, through it all. When you wait, when you hurt, the world and those you love can seem removed, distant, their touch deadened. But those days were over. Parents, siblings, and friends were now beside us, basking in the glory of God's stunning miracle.

~

You might think it impossible that after being damaged by infertility, wounded by waiting and disappointment, that we would not at some point wonder if this was too good to be true. You might assume that somewhere in the back of our minds, like an implanted aneurism of doubt waiting to burst, was a voice stating that our lot in life was not to rejoice, but to struggle. You might imagine this voice whispered that our child would die, that it would not take a single breath on this earth. That this miracle was all a cosmic ruse to set us up, bait us into happiness, then crush us. And you'd be right. We absolutely battled these fears. Especially Julia. It was not uncommon in that summer, that as I laid with my head planted on her stomach, her lips would suddenly begin to quiver, her eyes start to water, and she would unload these very concerns. Oh, but my answer was so easy! To be honest, I actually enjoyed this scrutiny. That may sound strange, but until you've spent month after month watching your wife wail out questions to God while your helpless mouth is slammed shut, answers evaporating out of sheer fragility before they form in your throat, you won't know the pleasure of having free lips to reply with credible, applicable encouragement. My words were always simple and always alleviating: "There is no way God would give us this miracle just to take it away." And the best part? I knew I was right. I felt it like an impenetrable coating on my heart, impossible to efface. Julia felt it too. We would smile at the nonsense of such stupid distress, laugh at what it must be like for God to watch his two neurotic children waste time worrying about losing the very miracle only he could create. I would then kiss her stomach repeatedly, murmur jokes and gibes and tender visions of all that life in our home would have in store for this little being.

Soon, these fears grew feeble and these evil whispers faded. By the time Julia was 34 weeks pregnant, and the doctor had continually counted her and the baby as healthy and whole, we completely let go, dove in to the deep end of our dream, and for the first time, didn't think twice about the possibility of drowning. Julia was so mesmerizing at her baby shower. I wish I could describe it. But some things won't allow words to limit them - Julia at eight months pregnant, showered with gifts she had thought she was destined never to receive, is one of them. We waited with bated breath for our baby to be born into the world. We had decided to forego finding out the sex, so I painted the nursery a weightless green.

CHAPTER SIX

- DISAPPEARING -

This is where we must begin: incommensurate pain,
nothing you can hope to finger
into exposition, nothing you can
cover up. A fault -
unacceptable and broad as life - gapes
at your feet, and the thin soil you stand
upon is giving way.

- Scott Cairns, from 'Disciplinary Treatises'

It was a warm Monday night at the end of August; not unlike the evening nearly three years previous when this whole journey started in a grocery store parking lot. Julia and I were sitting on our bed, talking and laughing; as always, I had my head propped on her now enormous orb of a belly. We were only a few short weeks away from meeting our first born child, so naturally, I was trying my best to hold an intimate conversation with him or her. I did this quite often - I would nuzzle in, plant my lips against Julia's stomach, maybe even push her face away to ensure privacy, and whisper to my child, ever so sweetly, "Kick me in the face." Previewing my positive influence as a father. I reassured Julia that my baby would leave the womb knowing how to defend itself. Sure enough, after enough goading, the kick would come - so strong, so healthy, like my kid was already in cahoots with me, already eager to please, already in love.

I also remember a playful argument about names ensuing. I really liked the name Will if we had a boy. However, Julia had had a conversation with her parents, and they immediately started claiming nicknames - her dad wanted to call him Willy, and as a person who has never been into people calling me Danny, I was not supportive. But then her mom escalated things with the nickname "Wee Willy". So of course I was bombarded with flash-forward nightmares of our son cowering in the corner of a middle school locker room with the other boys chanting "Wee Willy" while he silently hated us. Julia and I were laughing so hard. I wish so badly I could describe how tranquil these moments were for me. I cannot. It is one of the great sadnesses of human experience - tragedy steals the accuracy and purity of your vocabulary, and never gives them back.

The next morning, I went to work as usual. I taught first period. Afterwards, Julia called me. Her voice was shaky and hollowed out by fear. She told me she hadn't felt the baby move that morning. I told her not to worry. She tried all her normal tricks to rouse the baby - a shower, a twist of the hips, a carbonated drink - nothing. I encouraged her that the baby was simply taking a nap, no doubt tuckered out from the previous night's tae-kwon-do lesson. Nervous laughter. She had scheduled a doctor's appointment that morning anyway, and again, I told her everything would be fine.

An hour later, I was eating an early lunch with my good friend and co-worker when my phone rang. I picked it up. What I heard on the other end will haunt me until I leave this earth. It was first a strangled moan, a lacerated intake of breath; a chord of wailing more animal than human. Then Julia's voice as I had never heard it - hijacked, beaten, left for dead. Time dripped to nanoseconds as her words began to form. A single statement, barely audible: "We lost the baby." I can still hear the desperation oozing from the "What?!" I repeatedly yelled into the phone. Only wracked wailing on the other end. I lumbered out of the room, my legs went liquid, and I sank into a bench outside, the bulk of all the mourning that was to come rallying behind my eyes. Instantly the tears spilt forth like screaming passengers fleeing a sinking ship. Hyperventilation. Manic cries of "No!" and manic thoughts that everything can still be fine, things should be fine, things must be fine. My child is safe. My child will wake up. My child is from God. That which is from God is living, breathing, beautiful. Everything will be fine. These were the thoughts pulsating in my brain as I drove to the hospital. This is what I told myself as I burst through those office doors, accosted by the averted eyes of ashamed nurses and doctors. As I found my wife sitting lifeless in an abandoned room, quarantined, as if her calamity were contagious. Even as we wept together, even as we listened together to the monstrous emptiness of a silent ultrasound, even as the doctor told us that the child without a heartbeat inside Julia's womb was a girl. A little girl. My daughter. Even then, I wanted to deny it, this gruesome reality. I was still holding on to the illusion that we could get her back, that she would return to us, that this living nightmare would soon be over. It is akin to having your life savings in pennies dumped into a vast shoreline that is being punished by angry, ever-accelerating waves, and you are the madman diving in, nearly drowning in the current, trying to catch every coin. It is futile, you know; everywhere you look a piece of your dream, your heart, your hope sails out to sea, is swallowed up by depths unknown. But you refuse to fully taste the present, so you plunge in again, scoop up what you can, and shove it in pockets already torn through at the bottom.

~

I see my memory as an ever-growing train, each car representing a different scene, and I am the conductor. At any point, I can shoot backwards down the linking corridor and inhabit a certain car, a precise memory - I can sit down, take a look around, and see it all as clear as the current day. Naturally, the caboose is so far back it's nearly impossible to reach, but this I do not lament, for that is exactly what it is: natural. What is arrestingly unnatural is what happens to the train when life as you know it is unexpectedly traumatized, obliterated. These memories of my daughter's death, this specific collection of cars, have been violently derailed, flipped into a ditch, and disconnected from one another. Some exploded on contact, some have burned up slowly - they exist now only as charred masses I can never step into again. Perhaps this is a post-traumatic gift, a built-in immunity to viewing the complete dimensions of what happened. All I am left with, then, is a graveyard of beleaguered boxcars; so to camp down inside them, I must exit the train of my memory altogether, step outside normal space and time, outside customary recollection, and can only confront each car separately as a frightening metal cage lying on its side, destined never to right itself on the track.

~

I am on my knees in my bedroom. The pulse of Julia weeping nearby pounds in my ears. My head hangs loosely between my legs, and my sobs involuntarily elevate my spine, like steady puffs of air filling a windbag. It is easily the tenth location in our house where my bones have hollowed and caved, and I've lost all ability to stand. An odd realization: In the first hours of a sudden tragedy, there seems to be a feverish restlessness in your veins, like your body simultaneously desires to bury itself alive and run away to jump off a cliff - thus, you stop then start, crumble then crawl, go mute then moan, searching for nothing then searching for everything. I see Julia bent over our couch, nearly vomiting out the plague of misery scattering inside her. I am run over for the first time by the hideous thought: "My sweet daughter is dead inside my wife's womb." And my legs once more evaporate, my head plummets like an anvil, and my wailing erupts from depths darker than I knew existed inside my body.

Next, there are family members arriving. One by one they step through our door as frightened children enter a pitch-black cave, envisioning the horrors their meager flashlights will expose. What they find is their daughter, their son, their sister, their brother as they have never seen them. What they see is ashen, grey human beings barely breathing. And they feel for the first time the gravity of their own debilitating fear. Fear that is already lodging itself behind the sadness and the helplessness. It is the fear that bites deep and barks loudly, "They will never come back. They are lost forever." And with each reunion, with each multi-minute embrace, new bawling bellows out, fresh tears fall over old, and despair more potent than before distances us all further from the delusion that this will ever be redeemed. Strangely enough, I was struck then with a strong sense of remorse, and I could only exhale a strained "I'm sorry" to each loved one. Of course it was true, I was so very sorry. Sorry they were losing a granddaughter before they ever met her, sorry they were forced to mourn the life of a niece they would never get to know. Sorry that this disaster had detonated in the center of our family, our lives, our dreams. But there was more. I think I was sorry that we all lived on this planet. I think I was apologizing that the human condition was more hideous than I could have ever imagined, that there was an evil here that perhaps could not be overthrown. And maybe that is what is really at the heart of it, if I'm totally honest. Maybe I was saying sorry for God. Because when I saw each family member weep bitter tears as they let a quaking hand drift atop then touch Julia's stomach, and I saw the muscles in their face tighten and torque in shared anguish, maybe what was welling inside me was the awful speculation that a world this broken could never exist if it was truly created by a good God.

~

I am in a stark-white hallway. My mother-in-law sits beside me. Silence reigns save the sound of the doctors scrubbing in nearby, making small talk in low voices. As I half-listen to them, I am stabbed for the first time with a realization that will continually wound me over the next several months: People move on with their lives. Time, like a thieving bastard, keeps moving, keeps taking. Cordial conversations in sterilized hospital hallways continue. Truth: there are other things to talk about except your misfortune. And it kills you.

Our doctor steps over beside us. I do not look up, only trace the laces on his tennis shoes. He speaks, but there is no textbook that has prepared him for this one-sided interaction. As if this wasn't enough, Julia is not just any patient. She is a nurse at this hospital; she is one of them, she is beloved and cherished - the death of her seemingly healthy daughter who was known by all as a miracle shatters the very foundation of this maternity unit. All are crying with her. And when he steps into that operating room, this will be the most crushing C-section her doctor will ever perform. Again, I feel that remorse. I do not want him to blame himself, I do not want him to question whether he could have caught something and saved our daughter's life. I think I just want him to be quiet. What is creeping up inside me is the first bout of the paralyzing numbness of grief. Perhaps numbness is not the best word, for that would imply that you cannot feel it, and that is certainly not the case. It is more like subtly poisonous novocaine injected behind your eye balls, in your temples, and at the base of your neck. It seeps into your brain. Murders each thought before it forms. Is this a gift, to lose the ability to categorize or qualify what you're experiencing? Maybe. I think that's why during a tragedy and the following days, months, and years, numbness is such an attractive, alluring friend. But you find, as with so many other coping agents, that it deceives and deserts you, for the numbness is, at the end of the day, only a reminder that you have been removed from the land of the living, and your heart and soul are simply hiding away until the day you get to die.

~

In the operating room, I begged God to raise her from the dead. Crazy? I didn't think so. I pleaded with the Almighty. My heart nearly dislodged with the force of yearning behind each appeal. I became a desperate, dime-store lawyer stating my case before what I hoped would be a fair and righteous judge. "Think of the Glory you would receive, Lord." I even presented him with potential scenarios, potential visions; tears streaming down the face of unbelievers as they fell to their knees and worshipped the God who raised our daughter back to life. Just think of it. To tell people, "Yes, she was declared dead. And now she lives." Would this not incite a revival? Would this not repair everything to wholeness again?

I tried an opposite tactic - wouldn't God's reputation take an enormous blow here? Wouldn't most people think, when they hear of our daughter's sudden passing, when they ponder its lack of rhyme or reason, and when they measure this against our heavy laden journey to conceive her, that God is malicious at worst and indifferent at best? Wouldn't this even rob people of their salvation, if only because they would decide once and for all that God is the most callous of absentee landlords? "But good news!" I told him, "You can turn it all around and save everything - my daughter's life and your notoriety."

During the most stifling progressions in the operating room, when I was sure I would pass out from the pressure of such a heinous picture unfolding before me, I drifted into a last-ditch daydream born out of the remembrance that God had done this before; that is, raising someone from the dead. I told him I knew how easy it was for him to do, so I fabricated in my mind our own Lazarus raising. It goes something like this: I look over to the door. Jesus himself is slipping into the room, and only I can see him. He offers the most gracious of smiles. But it disappears when he gets his bearings, when he sees the atrocity on the table, as if he is discovering it for the first time. I sprint to him, clutch his shoulders, shake them, and cry, "Why did you not come earlier?! Why did you not save her?" And he does the most curious, most human of things. He weeps. Real tears. We cry together, like two brothers. After a few minutes, he lifts his head - there is a peace on his face that is otherworldly, supremely serene. He glides past me to the table and grazes a gentle hand over Julia's forehead. Just as our daughter is lifted from the womb, he simply touches her frail chest, whispers a loving word, and her little heart lifts off, takes flight. Color returns, and she fills the room with her healthy cries. The doctor nearly drops her, this living, breathing miracle. And we all laugh and cry and laugh some more as Jesus laughs and cries with us. Can you imagine it? This is what I prayed for in those last seconds before they took her out. This is what I continued to beg God for as she was brought forth, as vicious silence infected the room, as they announced her time of death, and as the realization hit home: to save her would be nothing for God and everything to me, and yet he had decided not to. I have often wondered if this must be a grief even God finds difficult to swallow - one of his children being blotted out by sorrow, appealing to his infinite power, begging for a miracle, and receiving a silent NO that wrecks so completely the very heart he wishes to protect.

We had only a few hours to hold our daughter. These images I keep for myself - they are the tiny remnants of a treasure ripped from the earth, reserved for eternity. But in short, it was a father falling in love with his daughter. I heard someone say once about their own lost child: "We did not get to love her for a lifetime, but we loved her a lifetime's worth." This is what seized me so violently in our hospital room. A lifetime's worth of love crashing into me and through me - love that cradles, changes diapers, makes funny faces; love that teaches to walk, to read, to say please and thank you; love that drops off at school, takes to church, introduces Jesus; love that threatens boyfriends, affirms her beauty always, and one day walks her down the aisle. There is more, of course, but that is the problem. I have decades of specific ways in which I was to love my daughter and nowhere to put them. So the malignant mass of what-ifs remains, and with every passing day, the shape and clarity of it dissipate while its density multiplies. We gave her a name. It was Emma Jo.

~

What of God's seeming truancy? Is this not the sharpest heartache? The cruelest joke of all? I have been scared many times in my life. I have felt the pit in my stomach sink and contort as fear overcomes. But never as it overcame me in those first few days. This is because I asked God "why?" and he did not answer. No audible word. No gentle whisper from the Holy Spirit. Not even a stiff breeze to let me know he was there. Just cold, dead nothingness. I remember stepping outside our apartment one of those first nights. Suddenly aware of the stars, the presumed handiwork of God. Constellations, planets, supposed order out of chaos. And I remember weathering the deepest wave of fear that I had been lied to all my life - that even the stars are haphazardly displaced, random and unloved, burning out alone in a universe without a maker.

In a letter written weeks later, Julia wrote this:

Our road to parenthood has been much like a battleground. For two and a half years prior to my pregnancy, we dodged the bullets of despair and discouragement related to infertility, eventually being led on to adoption. We heeded instruction from the Captain, we obeyed even when we didn't understand the orders, and ultimately we submitted our own ideas of how things should work. While at times there was intense struggle in our souls, we experienced something in our faith that cannot be found without total dependence on our Savior. God made himself more real; He gave us joy as we walked through these trials alongside Him. This joy of following Him soon replaced the anguish of not having a child. There was a momentum and we were rolling with it full steam. And then, in his is grace, a surprise came our way. We became pregnant with Emma. It all made sense. It was as if we finally got clarity as to why the road leading up to this had taken so long. It felt like we had arrived on safe ground.

Our baby was formed by the Hands of God, in his perfect timing, and the years of struggle were a small price compared to the blessing of being parents to little Emma. I enjoyed 34 weeks with my baby. I knew her likes and dislikes. I knew what time of day she took her best nap. I knew the outline of her perfect body as she stretched up against mine. I knew how often she got hiccups and I knew how much she loved to hear her daddy's voice. I knew her. She was my child and I could not wait to meet her. Pregnancy was a gift, and I cherished it.

On August 31st, our life was shattered into a million pieces. The atomic bomb in the war we thought was over was dropped on our home camp. Our daughter was born into heaven in the wee hours of the night. The hands that created her were the same hands she ran into that

Tuesday morning. What was left on earth was complete and utter devastation. The suffocating reality of such tragedy, such loss was unfathomable.

Every dream of our future felt like it died that day and now we were living in a nightmare. How could this be happening? This cannot be real. We were fine on Monday. She was active, I felt great. All I could think was, 'this cannot be my life.' My greatest fear had become the essence of my existence.

On September 1st I delivered Emma Jo. She was beautiful, and we could not have loved her more. Not a single flaw on that perfect face. Some described her as a long, lanky lady, weighing 5 lbs 4.3 oz and measuring 21" long. As I stared at her tiny rose bud lips and button nose I wept. I wept for everything we had lost. Not a single thing makes sense. We had prepared a room for her and now it lay empty. Why were we meeting her for the first time, and already having to say goodbye? A child should not die before her parents. This is brokenness.

CHAPTER SEVEN

- BURNING -

"Don't tell me the moon is shining; show me the glint of light on broken glass."

- Anton Chekhov

2nd Corinthians 4:8 says, "We are afflicted in every way, but not crushed; perplexed, but not driven to despair; persecuted, but not forsaken; struck down but not destroyed." And yet in every way I felt crushed, I felt despair, I felt forsaken, and I felt destroyed. I comprehended now that I had but whiffed the nauseating scent of suffering up to this point. Childhood dysfunction, relational strains, even the isolating defeat of infertility, were nothing compared to this. This was a species of mourning unmatched - so overwhelming that your brain is resistant to processing the amplitude of it, and so the affliction must burrow elsewhere, everywhere. Not a single exhale passed without it's taste on my lips. And I was supposed to agree with Paul that I am not destroyed?

I refused to read my Bible in those first days. I judged it a clumsy diary of poems and love letters and homage paid to a Creator who did not care for what he crafted. It was outdated, irrelevant, even mocking; for what good was an old script about God's redemption to a fresh pain that seemed absent of that very atonement? Instead of reading about how he had shown himself to others, I kept begging Jesus to show himself to ME. I was desperate to see him. Feel him. Know him. In any way or any place. See, it never felt viable to conclude that there was no God because of this tragedy. I say this strictly as a crushed human being, not as some product of religious predilections or disciple of hardheaded fanaticism; I say it as a person with a soul who knows in his depths, despite being mired in this atrocity, that there is a Being above and beyond what is seen. But what did feel horrifyingly viable, even justified, was questioning and scrutinizing and interrogating at every level this Biblical proposition: "The Lord is near to the brokenhearted and saves the crushed in spirit." I wanted to believe it. No, I wanted to know it. I wanted clarification once and for all as to how this God of mine interacted with humanity. Especially in those times when all is lost, and the only otherworldly communication you can imagine is the devil's laughter. And I must testify that God did show himself to me. But not through an audible voice. Not through an ethereal touch. But through the love and care of his people.

~

Grief at this magnitude is like you are strapped to a chair, alone in an empty room, in a house in the middle of the woods. And the house is burning down. The tower of fire is devouring every square foot. You try to rip and writhe free, but you can't. You have been deserted - the flames are rising, and the torture is unbearable. Outside, there are friends and loved ones who have arrived. Some offer their condolences; write comforting cards and say that they are praying for you. It's as though they are holding those miniature fire extinguishers, emitting their small puff of coolant on the roaring fire. From your lonely chair, you hear them faintly - it comforts you to know that they are trying. But you're still shackled, abandoned in blazing flames that will not be quenched. There are others; they haul buckets of water to the scene. Still others ready a hose. And everyone is desperately trying to make these flames disappear. They weep empathetic tears, because they know that inside that house, you are screaming, crying, burning, and dying away. They're certain they are useless, because despite their efforts, the fire will not recede, and you remain in horrific agony.

But there are a few who choose a different role. Only a few. They slowly split the crowd of people working to extinguish the fire, and they're strangely silent, strangely calm. They take their first step up the front stairs and greet the hot breath of angry flames. Yet they continue walking to the front door. They pry it open - the fire leaps onto their skin, singes deep, and though the agony is far worse than they could've fathomed, they stumble inside. Before long, they are in that isolated room, nearly collapsed, draped in the ocean of flames it took to get near you. Finally, they grasp a chair and set it right next to yours. They sit down without saying a word. And they burn beside you.

~

I am convinced that the people who burned alongside us in those first weeks; those whose backs strained under the shared weight of mutual loss, whose faces weathered from communal tears, those who served and soothed and comforted us as the hands and feet of Christ; it was they who saved our lives and our faith. They were my first proof that not only was Jesus acquainted with grief, not only was he near to the brokenhearted, but that he comforts us in our darkest days. I knew now that through his people, he dwells in the very black holes that have been ripped out of our universe and gives them light, and love, and life.

Perhaps you are skeptical about this, as I have been. Perhaps you think that people are naturally good, naturally self-sacrificing, and naturally able to share the burdens of those that are enduring catastrophes. They are simply responding to an obvious need with obvious help. Perhaps, in the end, you believe that the idea that God would choose to comfort, to love, and to reveal himself through humanity, his flawed creation, is a weak and half-hearted measure. I do not think it so. It was the most tremendous thing - I begged God for evidence of his love, his presence, and that is exactly what he gave me. And when I read 1 John 4:12, it is confirmed: "No one has ever seen God. But if we love each other, God lives in us, and his love is brought to full expression in us." This verse saturates my heart with a sweet reprieve from all the questioning and doubting about how God shows up for his people. First, admission: "No one has ever seen God." This is not a sad realization to me. It is the exact opposite, simply because it feels honest - at no time during these horrific days and weeks did I ever see God. Second, explanation: "But if we love each other, God lives in us, and his love is brought to full expression in us." Full expression. Not a muffled utterance of God, not a smoky image out of reach, but a full expression. An expression that can be felt, touched, heard; a complete manifestation of God that comforts, declares truth, and serves in such a way that offers present soothing and the hint of future healing. And most essential, these full expressions stir your affections for Christ; they draw you closer and closer to God, which, though you may not know or understand or even forgive him for what he has allowed, softens something inside you and heats what is growing cold.

It was the love of his people that compelled me to seek more of him. This is no small revelation. Understand, please, that I was not drawn to God through words alone. No card, however eloquently written, convinced me of God's nearness. No pledge of prayer, though clearly sincere, gave me a hope that surpassed my circumstances. No passing words, no prepared phrase, no comfortably distant advice or solitary suggestion or, worst of all, explanation for why all of this happened, gave me the confirming evidence that God is beside me in this heartache. By itself, no anecdote of someone else's redemption, someone else's intimacy with a loving God prompted me to seek God's face. No biblical argument, however viable, convinced me God wanted to lift my face from the dirt. In fact, to hear a drawn out contention of why I should still love and trust in God from a person who refuses to taste the mud in their mouth, who declines to let the disease that is killing me infect them too, only served to harden my heart toward Jesus. For what comfort are even the most biblical words from a passing motorist to a man bleeding to death in the street?

Henri Nouwen explains it well: "When we honestly ask ourselves which person in our lives means the most to us, we often find that it is those who, instead of giving advice, solutions, or cures, have chosen rather to share our pain and touch our wounds with a warm and tender hand. The friend who can be silent with us in a moment of despair or confusion, who can stay with us in an hour of grief and bereavement, who can tolerate not knowing, not curing, not healing and face with us the reality of our powerlessness, that is a friend who cares." [2] I am

[2] Nouwen, Henri. *The Road to Daybreak: A Spiritual Journey*. Doubleday. 1988.

convinced that no theological exegesis, however viable, can, by itself, persuade that life returns to withered bodies, that God is lovingly, desperately, and untiringly pursuing humanity. This is precisely because God actually intends to effectuate his powerful presence through human beings. All around us, there are those who are burning in their chairs. I wonder if we do not do more damage by simply talking so much. I wonder if by proclaiming our enduring love for those being overwhelmed by flames only to run at the first hint of heat, by pointing from our personal pulpits to a Jesus we refuse to thoroughly embody, if we do not provoke more flames than we quench.

~

I met a man named Jerry once on a short-term missions trip to Mexico. He has run a prison ministry for over twenty years in the city of Mexicali. Here's what I witnessed: He does not sweep inside the gates and gather all the inmates so that he might preach to them from a guard tower. He does not hand out Bibles, quote Jesus, then say, "Think about it," only to then turn around and head back to his less troubled life. No, he plays soccer and basketball with murderers. He laughs, and sweats, and roughhouses with rapists. He laments and comforts and looks into the eyes of drug lords. He is unreservedly inclusive to a people group defined by their exclusion from society, by their destiny to be labeled modern-day lepers. One night, as I talked with Jerry about his work in the prisons, I asked him about this very thing; about how we as Christians might truly show the love of Christ. He became very serious, even grave. He looked me in the eye, put a hand on my shoulder, and drew me closer. He said, "Jesus' words changed people's lives. But listen to me. It was never words alone. He touched the leper. Do you understand me? He, the God of the universe, touched the leper. And we must do the same."

Grief is leprosy. You are convinced that you have been spit out to the edges of a city where evil shadows are your shelter and excruciating pain is the only evidence that you still exist. But when you see that person who has walked miles to meet you, when they sit down with you, when they let their smooth skin touch your cracked, oozing sores, when they draw their clean face to your ravaged complexion and allow their tears to mix with yours, you become equally human, equally alive. And this, to the outcast, is the sweetest offering; they are, for the first time, looking into the loving eyes of God.

So this was my first turning point. My first shift. I had, through the care of others, come to believe God was present. The love of these people persuaded me to read scripture, listen to sermons, and pray rightly for the first time after losing my only child. In short, they compelled me to seek more truth. However, being compelled to seek truth is one thing, stomaching it is something else entirely.

CHAPTER EIGHT

- BATTLING -

"You never know how much you really believe anything until its truth or falsehood becomes a matter of life and death to you."

- C.S. Lewis

It is my experience that the second a tragedy occurs, a cosmic war between truth and falsehood commences in every corner of the torn heart. Immediately, the armies of lies and cynicism, taking advantage of this dire reality, bolster their ranks and attack, while the side of truth and hope, eager to transcend these horrifying circumstances, scramble to attention and fight back. In short, it is a bloody clash between God and the devil, with your soul as the spoils. True, you might say this is a struggle both opponents are continually engaged in, no matter the person and no matter the situation; but on the heels of death and loss, legions on both sides grow louder and fiercer than they've ever been before. And for all those in grief, this exhausting conflict rages on every minute, every hour, and every day for months and even years - it is never concluded in a single battle. It is my belief, however, that the God of all truth, the God that proffers peace and joy, wins the day.

The Bible is dead vs. The Bible is alive

The first time I opened a Bible after losing Emma, I prayed a short, simple prayer: "God, show me something in this book that feels true." That's all I said, and not without a tone of instigation. It was more than a dare, more than a demand - it was, whether right or wrong, a test that would determine my future dedication to God. I was not concerned necessarily with truth that had already been agreed upon for generations by other people, or even what felt authentic and verifiable about the love I had received from others. If I can be brutally honest, I was not interested in verses that spoke of God's love, his faithfulness, or how everything works out for good. That could not possibly be my starting point, for my wrecked heart did not reside there. And I certainly wasn't interested in verses that spoke of God's sovereignty, his fairness, or his righteous judgment. It all felt bitter, slippery, and false. What I desired more than anything else were words in this book that felt real to me; right now. Words that were as alive as everyone claimed they were. Never in my life had I opened the Bible with such desperation; such groaning, aching desire to receive, above all, a true word from God. This is what he gave me:

Psalm 88

1 O Lord, God of my salvation,
  I cry out to you by day.
  I come to you at night.
2 Now hear my prayer;
  listen to my cry.
3 For my life is full of troubles,
  and death draws near.
4 I am as good as dead,
  like a strong man with no strength left.
5 They have left me among the dead,
  and I lie like a corpse in a grave.
  I am forgotten,
  cut off from your care.
6 You have thrown me into the lowest pit,
  into the darkest depths.
7 Your anger weighs me down;
  with wave after wave you have engulfed me.
8 You have driven my friends away
  by making me repulsive to them.
  I am in a trap with no way of escape.
9 My eyes are blinded by my tears.
  Each day I beg for your help, O Lord;
  I lift my hands to you for mercy.
10 Are your wonderful deeds of any use to the dead?

Do the dead rise up and praise you?
11 Can those in the grave declare your unfailing love?
Can they proclaim your faithfulness in the place of destruction?
12 Can the darkness speak of your wonderful deeds?
Can anyone in the land of forgetfulness talk about your righteousness?
13 O Lord, I cry out to you.
I will keep on pleading day by day.
14 O Lord, why do you reject me?
Why do you turn your face from me?
15 I have been sick and close to death since my youth.
I stand helpless and desperate before your terrors.
16 Your fierce anger has overwhelmed me.
Your terrors have paralyzed me.
17 They swirl around me like floodwaters all day long.
They have engulfed me completely.
18 You have taken away my companions and loved ones.
Darkness is my closest friend.

The lie conceived in my heart after losing my daughter was that nothing in the Bible, that ancient script filled with out-of-touch commands and empty comforts, would ever be able to adequately speak to or articulate the sadness I was bearing. But when I read these words from the Psalmist, I heard my own heart's lament, my own soul's elegy. I heard a man who was "paralyzed", "engulfed", "overwhelmed", and "helpless". I heard a man who was legitimately questioning God - "Can those in the grave declare your unfailing love? Can the darkness speak of your wonderful deeds?" I heard a man who was too tortured to placate his audience or his God by turning the final prose into upbeat praise. He instead offers concluding lines that rip right to the core - "Darkness is my closest friend." Nothing felt more palpable, more authentic. I remember sitting around a table with my mom and dad, whimpering these brutal cries of the forsaken, and telling them how grateful I was for this Psalm. Yes, grateful. I had asked for something that felt true, and God had delivered. For weeks, this was the only scripture I read. Over and .over again, I would place myself shoulder to shoulder with the Psalmist and wail out my distress with him, question my Creator with him, and confess that darkness is my sole companion with him. Surprisingly, this breathed into me the faintest whisper of hope. For if God could comfort me with the gift of something clear and real in these days when I felt naked, blind, and discarded, perhaps he could meet and mold my heart in a way that would make me ready to receive more truth, more hope.

Something changed radically in the following weeks when I approached the Bible with this sense of urgency. I realized that for all of my life, I had opened the pages of scripture as though it were just a book, just words God would prefer if I read occasionally. But now? Now it was different. Now I was suffocating and these words were air. I would wake before the sun rose, tired from sleepless nights punctuated by weeping, and rip the pages open. I would say to God, "I can not make it through this day unless you speak to me right now. Please God, I beg you. Speak to me through this book so I can truly believe." And every day, he absolutely answered; so I kept reading, kept devouring his words, kept straining to discover his character, his nature, and his call on my shattered life. You see, I began to wonder, even then, if the reason the Bible had not seemed alive to me before had more to do with the fact that I was living a life that did not absolutely require it to save me, to comfort me, or to strengthen me. In other words, if I was choosing a comfortable existence in which I did not desperately need God, wasn't I forcing the Bible to be largely irrelevant? But now, through a tragedy I did not foresee and I would never choose, I was beginning to see that full dependence on God and full dependence on his word go hand in hand, and one without the other was the worst kind of counterfeit.

You are the exception vs. You are the rule

I owe more than I can ever repay to a man named Britt Merrick. He is the pastor at a church called Reality in Ventura, California. Not long after we lost Emma, I listened to a sermon that he gave entitled "Struck Down but Not Destroyed". The context is heartbreaking, but the message is incredible. Only a week before he spoke to the congregation, Britt was devastated by the news that his five year old daughter, Daisy, was diagnosed for a second time with cancer after the doctors found a tumor the size of a grapefruit in her abdomen. They had, as a family, already battled for over a year through Daisy's first bought with cancer and were looking toward a brighter future when this sudden and horrifying incident occurred. His words are raw and real, his truth and faith even more so.

I went for a run, and listened to the podcast. I wept through most of it, aware that I must have looked schizophrenic to each passerby. Much of what Britt talks about in the sermon strikes at the heart of every step of our journey - the disappointment of initial diagnosis, the agony of waiting, coupled with the beauty of knowing Christ more entirely in the midst of it, and finally, the heartbreaking bait and switch of celebrating a miraculous new season only to watch it evaporate in one brutal instant. He literally spoke to every aspect of our grief, but it was a single question that cut me from the inside out. I remember it so vividly because it was the first time after losing Emma that I felt the pang of conviction. It was the first time I experienced that familiar ache of being confronted, challenged, even rebuked. And it knocked the wind out of me. Here is what he said: "We've had to remind ourselves this week that what we're going through is not unique. When this happens, you feel alone. I was watching families come into church with their kids, and you just feel like everyone else is okay. Their kids are healthy, their kids are here. Why are we the only ones going through this? But that's never true. That's never true...My wife and I have had to look at each other and say, 'Kids die everyday. Parents lose children everyday.' And how selfish and wrong would it be to think that when my daughter is dying, that all of a sudden God isn't good? Thousands of children are dying every day. Was I to say God was good when it was their child who was dying? But to now somehow disbelieve that because it's my own child, how selfish and wrong and arrogant would that be?"[3]

My first reaction: How selfish and wrong and arrogant of God to convict me through this man's words. I had earned the right to look around me at all the blissful mothers and fathers and convince myself I was the only one wearing this crown of thorns. I had earned the right to completely ignore the cold fact that at the very moment I was mourning my daughter here in America, thousands upon thousands of mothers and fathers all over the globe were wailing for the same reason. I kept picturing a woman in Somalia, her child plagued by the fierce indifference of malnutrition and dying slowly in its mother's arms. What did that mother see when she looked to the sky? Were her tears not as heavy? Did they not burn with the salt of injustice? Were they not as real? I didn't want to admit it. What I wanted, what every person in difficulty desires, is the prerogative of self-pity. Is there anything more alluring in grief than self-pity? Self-pity affirms what you already feel in your gut; that you are all by yourself and you always will be. More attractive, though, is the fact that it gives you something tangible to

---

[3] Merrick, Britt. *Struck Down But Not Destroyed.* Reality Sermon. July, 2010.

do in the desert you've been relegated to; so instead of entertaining the idea of taking steps forward, self-pity offers a limitless to-do-list for the immovable griever, for there is truly no end to the ways in which you can contemplate how a hardship is terrible for you and you alone. And finally, self-pity, like the most spineless of confidants, echoes every momentarily satisfying sentiment your mind creates about your own personal unfairness and anger. But self-pity is fools gold. In fact, it is really just a blanket dipped in freezing water offered to a man dying of hypothermia. Though the blanket may be wrapped around him, it will do anything but comfort him - it will only speed his descent toward a lonely, bitter death. And I knew this even as I wept through Britt's sermon; that self-pity would only serve to describe the dimensions of my coffin instead of lifting its lid and leading me out.

My second reaction: Britt was right. "To now somehow disbelieve that because it's my own child, how selfish and wrong and arrogant would that be?" His rhetorical question was tearing a huge hole in my right to diminish the holiness and goodness of God. More disarming, though, was that it swiftly carried me to the most important of decisions. I acknowledged that I had believed God was holy before Emma died. I had proclaimed his goodness everywhere - his loyalty through infertility, his grace in leading us to adoption, and his power in providing our miracle baby. And all that time, as I shouted his glorious name from the rooftops, I knew that babies were dying, gross oppression reigned, and senseless evil flourished all over the world. However, I still believed beyond any doubt that I served a loving God. A sovereign God. But now that I was numbered as one of those who suffer, suddenly I was questioning everything God said about himself. And it convicted me. Though I hated it, I was punched in the face with my humanity, my limited understanding, my inability to grasp or even judge the character of God. I had been brought to a choice, right here, right now. Either God was always good, despite any hardship inflicted upon me, or God was never good, precisely because people everywhere unjustly suffer the loss of everything they hold dear. Believe me, I did not like that I even had to make this choice. This is one of the most frustrating aspects of grief. You would gladly suspend your right to free will, would welcome God to force himself upon you, would celebrate the respite from voluntary faith, but it is not so. You are forced instead to maintain your own independent choice, about whom or what you are to follow or renounce, despite the fact that choice is exactly what was stolen from you in this tragedy you are enduring.

But I can testify that God's grace covers this completely. That day, collapsed on the grass, I decided to choose God. Somehow my choice to believe in God's eternal goodness did not feel like a begrudging resignation; it did not feel like giving up. Not another bitter ending, but beginning anew. Like I was choosing life. And I was seized by a distinct sense that my faith had reached a new and significant depth. That for the first time in my life, my faith was in fact absolutely real if only because it was absolutely necessary. A legitimate leap that transcended limited logic, defied human explanation. A choice to truly follow my God, despite the realities that swirled like a ruthless cyclone around me. And I felt his love. Knew his goodness. It was favor from a God who was pleased with me. An invigorating hint that when I die, and stand before him, he might say, "Well done my good and faithful servant." That though the groaning earth and my throbbing mind screamed to abandon him, I chose to follow God with everything I had left in me. This felt like privilege, like unblighted breath in my lungs. And the greatest comfort? I did not feel alone. This, I think, is the most significant of victories for God's truth, because I know beyond all doubt that the most grievous and yet most potent lie the enemy uses against those who suffer is that they are doing it alone, that no one can relate to their pain, that they have been shunned and neglected while everyone else moves on. But I know this is not the truth; my strengthened soul tells me so. And the Bible, as it always has, gives the greatest sense of reinforcement in this regard. My eyes were opened to all those who have suffered and nonetheless sing out with Jeremiah, "'The Lord is my portion,' says my soul, 'Therefore I have hope in Him.'" In almost every book of scripture, I now related to and received strength from men and women who were confronted with the same decision amidst their own suffering, and chose with confidence the God who upheld them. I was suddenly beside Job screaming out, "Though you slay me, I will hope in You." I was, with cracked ribs and torn flesh, weathering the stones with Stephen, all the while fastening my eyes to heaven, seeing the Son of Man in all his glory. I received with gladness the letter from Paul, exhorting me with these words: "For the more we suffer for Christ, the more God will shower us with his comfort through Christ...you can patiently endure the same things we suffer. We are confident that as you share in our sufferings, you will also share in the comfort God gives us." And finally, I fell to my face beside Jesus in the garden of Gethsemane, sweating drops of blood and crying, "My soul is crushed with grief to the point of death," and though I too desired this cup to pass by me, I could now match his faithful words to the Father, "I want your will to be done, not mine."

1 Peter 4: 12-13 says, "Beloved, do not be surprised at the fiery trial when it comes upon you to test you, as though something strange were happening to you. But rejoice insofar as you share Christ's sufferings, that you may also rejoice and be glad when his glory is revealed." I am struck by the use of the phrase, "when it comes upon you." This is because it does not say, "if it comes upon you"; it says "when". This strikes me mainly because it reminds me of a very similar lie vying for victory in my heart and mind. That is, that I as a Christian should not have to suffer. In fact, my goal in life should be to avoid suffering at all costs. I should plan, and scheme, and control my existence and that of my family in such a way as to protect myself and those I love from difficulties,

because I far too easily convince myself that the biggest blessing I can apprehend on this earth is the absence of pain. The absence of tears. The absence of death. Honestly, I do not think this desire is so unreasonable. After all, God designed our souls to function in this way. When I read in Revelation about a new heaven and new earth, I am bombarded by images of cheeks without tears, bodies without bruises; worship and wellness and walking without hardship. Is it so surprising, then, that as we stumble through this life on a planet crippled by sin, our hearts would naturally gravitate toward the physical comfort, emotional pleasure, and lack of misery our souls seem designed to eternally rest in? But this elevation of comfort is the most alluring falsehood. The Bible offers the opposite truth: that while we are still living on this earth, we are not to avoid suffering but instead expect it; and more importantly, we are to rejoice in it, for it is through that suffering that the glory of God is revealed to and through us. So as I looked around me, at faithful servants of Christ like Britt, I knew with certainty that I, as a Christian who was hurting so badly, was in no way an exception. I was most certainly the rule. And that truth personally invited me to take part in the narrative I saw replaying over and over again in the scriptures - simply, that the follower of Christ inevitably suffers; but forever and always, the good God of the universe comforts him, strengthens his soul, and draws him into a love he has never known.

God makes mistakes vs. God is sovereign

I have heard of men and women who, after being blind-sided by a great loss, do not ask God 'why?'. Their faith in God's sovereignty, his flawless plan, is such that they are not compelled to ask this question. I am not one of those people. In fact, I have at times been more than a little bothered by these all-stars of blind belief. Their declarations felt forced to me, like they had been pushed off a cliff, but rather than screaming bloody murder, they were gleefully bellowing out, "See!? God's plan is good! He wants me to fly!" And as an onlooker, I wanted to shout back, "No buddy, you're falling face first into jagged rocks." The surface source of this cynicism is simple: jealousy. I was envious of those who seemed to completely understand the world, with all its backward mysteries that remained unsolved to me; those whose faith was stronger, immovable, indestructible. But the root of my distrust with these people and their transcendence of the bankrupt 'why?' I woke with every morning went so much deeper than jealousy. It went to that place in my heart where there is one question that is always shrieking out to God, though I try to muzzle it often. It is not simply 'why?'; it is closer to this: "Did you make a mistake?"

First, for a few fleeting days, I saw my daughter's death as a punishment. I was sure that God, never more wrathful than in that moment, had decided he'd finally had enough of my defiant sin, my wicked heart, and my insistence on returning to my own vomit. He was, therefore, dolling out his anger now as payment for those trespasses, as a way to show that he, the God of the universe, would not be trifled with. I don't think there is a more soul-shattering way to view God. And I am so thankful that early on, I was restored by this truth: When Jesus Christ died on the cross, he boldly proclaimed, "It is finished." The weight of and wrath for all sin, past and present and future, was heaped upon the Son of God, so that those who call him Lord might be saved from eternal punishment. I knew this to be true. So to believe that God was punishing me now meant I was proclaiming Jesus Christ a liar. I was saying that in actuality it was not finished. It meant I believed that on that day when the sky crashed to blackness, as the bloodied Christ was crucified, God had somehow pocketed a handful of wrath and saved it just for me. I knew that to believe this meant to divorce the Gospel, and by doing so, to split irrevocably from God. This I could never do. But the devil is the shrewdest of opponents, for he gave up on that tactic quickly, and shifted to another, more substantial ploy. Thus, the lie took shape and the case was made: "Your God makes mistakes." And the evidence he presented? Reality. How could there not be a strong belief in me that God was in fact preoccupied when Emma breathed her last? How could I not cast God as an ambulance driver who was startled from sleep by our emergency bell in the cold of night, unaware he was supposed to be on duty? How could I not envision him nervously repeating "No,

No, No," as he ripped through traffic with sirens blazing, picture him bent over my daughter at the scene of the accident, face drenched with sweat and tears, refusing to stop CPR as we onlookers bowed our heads in silence with the malicious resignation that he had made a terrible mistake, that he was unable to save her? This could not be the better plan. There's absolutely no way this could be part of a better design. This sentiment haunts me even now, a ghostly whistle rising up from the unchecked corridors of my mind.

What is the sovereignty of God? It is a mystery. I know this is unsatisfying. What I want to do more than anything is lay out a logical argument for why these awful things happen. Look at it. Question it. God, how can it be logical to take a married couple who love you and deny them a child for two years, then lead them to adopt an Ethiopian child destined for deprivation, only to stop that process by giving them a biological child, bring peace and joy, but only so the tragedy of that child dying is more devastating and brutal? And you leave them with no children now, and no children on the horizon? How can this be the product of forethought? I want to answer for that. I want so badly to articulate to you a theologically air-tight explanation of where God lies in the hazy space between punishment and discipline, between what is deliberate and what is allowed, between what is planned and what is the natural outcome of a sinful world. A wiser man might have better answers. But this I do know; that belief in God's sovereignty is absolutely necessary.

Without it, we will suffocate under the weight of unexplainable circumstances.

Above all, believing in the sovereignty of God is a letting go. What falls from your clutches? The right to say how God should govern the universe. That is it, and that is all. We reach the precipice of logic, step out into that treacherous chasm between knowable earth and unknowable heaven, all the while wearied by intense doubt - the last stronghold of minds that were created to comprehend, now forced to embrace their inability to do so. For we will never have and we will never know the mind of God. We will never understand completely his ways. Isaiah 55: 8-10 makes this clear, "'My thoughts are nothing like your thoughts,' says the Lord. 'And my ways are far beyond anything you could imagine. For just as the heavens are higher than the earth, so my ways are higher than your ways and my thoughts higher than your thoughts.'" We are the clay and he is the potter, and though we pitch to him very preferred ways we'd like to be molded, he is the renowned sculptor whose talent is genius, love is perfect, and design is most beautiful. But nevertheless, as a skeptic, I am often discouraged by the fact that God would form our minds to be only intelligent enough to conceive that he denied us the power to fully conceive him. This feels twisted in some way. But out of this rises a crystal clear understanding of what it means to have faith. To believe that which we cannot, in spite of how hard we try, ever explain adequately. This I do know: In the end, everything on this earth that we put complete trust in will fail us, will forsake us, will fade to ashes. God is not so. He is above all. He is eternal. The greater danger, I believe, is that it will instead be my trust in him that will falter, will leave, will decay to dust. Meanwhile, the truth of God's sovereignty, his perfect plan, will ring out to me, for me. And it is a song that, though distorted and disguised by the deafening noise of our current desolation, nevertheless rings true and clear in my soul, in the only place where the eternal melody can be heard. So my choice was simple: Will I refuse to acknowledge his song until I know all the words, or will I trust enough to sing along at the top of my lungs regardless?

God can't relate vs. God knows suffering

God seems fake to me if I cannot be known by him. More than that, he seems fake if I cannot feel known by him. It appeared plausible to me in those first weeks that in some ways, God is unable to understand the plight of humanity. He is all-knowing, all-powerful. He exists above and beyond the limits of time and space. He claims victory over the entire universe; a universe he created in six days. How could God ever understand the limitations and loneliness of miniscule humanity? I hear the retort; he created us so he knows us, inside and out. I believe that, as I believed it in Sunday school. But after losing Emma, I did not feel it. More specifically, it wasn't so much whether or not God could know my soul, and more a question of whether God had ever truly tasted this kind of disappointment; this absolute defeat. Could he really relate to me? The lie was simple: No. God cannot see through his own deity mask. Cannot loose himself from perfection. So even if he viewed what was happening to me in crystal clarity, even if he comforted me with his presence, he would perpetually perceive me and my loss as one who approaches even the most well-developed characters in a work of fiction. No doubt he is the keenest reader, the most empathetic and aware and loving reader, but he is above the novel nonetheless, unable to dip into the dirty pages, unable to flail side-by-side with human beings as they drown in the ink. Yes, he could see and understand my pain, but would he ever share the battered pulse of a heart that's lost everything it beats for?

Such were the questions that poisoned my fitful nights. But clarity comes in the morning, and not always through a declaration. Often, it comes as a question that by it's very nature infiltrates, exposes, and detonates the lie. This is the question I woke with: Is it perhaps you, father of a lost child, who cannot possibly comprehend the magnitude of grief God experienced at watching his only Son crucified? I had spent so much time dissecting God's comfortable remove from pitiful humanity and, subsequently, his inability to ever know just how pitiful we feel here, I had neglected to consider that an alternative existed - the possibility that we as human beings are, in the end, only readers ourselves, and we will never, ever begin to comprehend the desolation brought on by watching our only child digesting all the world's darkness as he hangs on a tree. You see, the thing that pierces my soul most is the idea that Emma suffered as she passed away. The thought that my innocent child may have struggled for oxygen, endured even a wisp of pain; this rips a hole right through me. So can I imagine? Can I imagine what it would be like to watch my only child beaten, mocked, scourged, and spit on? To watch my blameless child hung up as a murderer, nails pounded into his flesh, choking on the sheer gravity of torment? And can I imagine what it would feel like to know that as my child wails out to me, "Why have you forsaken me?", I must allow the grossest and most grievous sin to be poured over him like a mile-high wave of all that is evil? I cannot even come close.

Two truths emerged for me. One, God has tasted this heartache of mine. Two, I cannot fathom the agony he felt for having given his only son over to torture and death. Both of these provided great comfort to Julia and I. Not only could we trust and feel that God has possessed this pain, despite his deity, but we could also rejoice at the magnitude of God's sacrifice for us. I was given, because of losing my daughter, an accurate picture of what it really meant for God to send his only son to die on the cross for our sins. This ceased to be a Bible story. This ceased to be cheap grace. It became the most radical display of love I could comprehend. The omniscient God, releasing his only child to be fully human, knowing all along that he would be slaughtered in the most gruesome and horrific way, that he would ingest all and die for humanity's litany of sins, so that myself, Julia, sweet Emma and the rest of the world might have eternal life. Then there is the sweet redemption: Christ is resurrected. He is returned home. He is whole. And we are saved. This was the gift of God, both to all of his creation and to me crawling through grief - that through the cross, not only do we see a picture of God's immeasurable love and his intimate understanding of our wounds, but we also grasp a vision of resurrection, of things being made new, of hope reconciled to the hopeless. It is a foretaste of the future encouragement addressed by Paul: "What we suffer now is nothing compared to the glory he will reveal to us later."

Emma the greatest treasure
vs.
Christ the greatest treasure

Phillipians 3: 7-8 reads, "I once thought these things were valuable, but now I consider them worthless because of what Christ has done. Yes, everything else is worthless when compared with the infinite value of knowing Christ Jesus my Lord. For his sake I have discarded everything else, counting it all as garbage, so that I could gain Christ." This was the battle I avoided engaging. It was the climactic conflict my heart could not resolve. I read those words from Paul a month after we lost Emma. But as always, I had questions: How can I count Emma as garbage? How can I count the miracle that she was as worthless? Does that not deface and devalue her - strip from her the last remaining joy that is tied to her loving parents? Didn't you give this child as a gift? Were we not to give thanks and take comfort in this "gain"? I understood, technically, the value of Christ above all. But I wanted to know, finally, what it feels like to have all my joy, peace, and assurance wrapped up in "gaining Christ."

I believed now that Christ reveals himself through the sacrificial love of people. I believed now that the Bible is alive. I believed now that God grants the grace to rejoice in suffering. I believed now that God is sovereign, that he is never surprised. And I believed that he thoroughly understands the magnitude of my loss. That through his great sacrifice, I now have an eternal hope. But this? Emma counted as garbage? Even the thought felt akin to betrayal. So, even with the assurance of all these aforementioned truths, even with these victories over the devil's lies, there rose the question I kept hearing, in scripture and in my own heart, that was in fact the very question I most needed to answer. God's question to me, to every human being really, is simple: Do you love me most? Oh, how I avoided answering. What about Emma, I'd think. What about all this evil down here? Do you really expect me to love you, God, the only one I do not see, so much that I view all that I actually get to see as merely worthless? Again the question from him: Do you love me most?

I think we'd all like to declare that yes, even in the midst of our worst trials, of course we love Jesus the most.

I had so much reason to. From the moment our lives imploded, Jesus had poured so much love and comfort and truth over us, it was truly staggering. But did I, really? Behind all my confident words about God's goodness, underneath all the private prayers and public declarations that God's will be done come what may, wasn't there a point when Christ became no longer worth it? A point when I had to swallow the truth that although I may never admit it, ultimately there was someone or something else worth more to me than Christ. John Piper poses it this way:

> "If you could have heaven, with no sickness, and with all the friends you ever had on earth, and all the food you ever liked, and all the leisure activities you ever enjoyed, and all the natural beauties you ever saw, all the physical pleasures you ever tasted, and no human conflict or any natural disasters, could you be satisfied with heaven, if Christ were not there?"[4]

Now let me restate it in the unique way my heart heard it:

> "If you could have heaven, with no sickness, and with all the friends you ever had on earth, and all the food you ever liked, and all the leisure activities you ever enjoyed, and all the natural beauties you ever saw, all the physical pleasures you ever tasted, and no human conflict or any natural disasters, *and eternity with your*

---

[4] Piper, John. *God is the Gospel*. Crossway. 2005.

beautiful, healthy, and whole daughter, could you be satisfied with heaven, if Christ were not there?"

I must confess that in those few hours at the hospital, when I held my daughter, when I wailed out, begging for God to lift her lungs with breath and her eyelids with sight, when I nearly collapsed at the might of love I felt for her, had this question been asked of me, I probably would have said yes. But again, Paul challenges this when he states: "Everything else is worthless when compared with the infinite value of knowing Christ Jesus my Lord. For his sake I have discarded everything else, counting it all as garbage, so that I could gain Christ." Really, this goes to the heart of why it is seems so absurd to follow Christ completely. Because if I'm honest, what I wanted for a long time was protection from a life that would require me to be left alone with Jesus. This is what Soren Kierkegaard means when he says, "If your ultimate and highest purpose is to have life made easy and sociable, then never have anything to do with Christianity. Flee from it, for it will do the very opposite; it will make your life difficult and do this precisely by making you alone before God."[5] Though I knew of Christ's infinite value, there was always a part of me that wanted to avoid the submission and humility and expected obedience that his presence demands. And where does this desire to flee from him originate? I think it comes from years of

[5] Kierkegaard, Soren. *Works of Love*. Harper Perennial Modern Classics. 2009.

practice. I know for a fact that Jesus is much more palatable as a figure who stays at the margins of my life. In that way, I can still pursue all that my heart actually values - comfort, safety, license, and power. Jesus plus my family, plus my plans and my purposes, is an easier pill to swallow - whole churches are built on this principle. But in the rush to insulate ourselves from difficulties, in the pursuit of our own gains in our own four walls, in our anxiety over and elimination of the possibility of suffering, we miss God as he was intended to be met. We do everything we can to protect ourselves from having to be totally naked and vulnerable and dependent on Christ alone, but the Bible shows us, and I have seen in my life, that it is the very instant we fall face to the pavement with all stripped away, that we truly find Christ, and in the valleys of our lives where he brings real nourishment. Where we are weakest that he is strongest. Where we are most destroyed that he is most complete. Where we feel most bereft of love that he shows us a love only he can give. This is real. It is true. And it allows for Julia and I to say along with Paul that everything is indeed worthless compared to the surpassing value of knowing Christ Jesus. It allows for us to repeat the words of the Psalmist, "Besides thee, I desire nothing on earth." That we can say to God, "Your love is better than life." Yes, we can profess that Jesus is worth more to us than Emma. So much more that though she obviously holds immense value in our temporal human hearts, when compared to the eternal worth of Jesus, she is reduced to her rightful place far beneath him. This is not betrayal. This is not a defeat or a giving up. This is a step into the open arms of Christ, who despite our doubts, deceits, and distress, will always love us enough to reveal that he is the greatest treasure we can ever discover. So when Jesus once and for all became our ultimate prize, we could no longer view the things of this world the same way. We couldn't view disasters, and heartache, and pain the same way. We couldn't digest our daughter's death in the same way. For all that befalls us, good and bad, is put in its right perspective when Jesus is our everything. Julia explains it well in the conclusion of the letter she wrote:

In the midst of this suffering, I don't pretend to understand. Sometimes I wish we had a clear answer to ease the ache of our broken hearts and the loneliness of our empty arms. Instead God has given us what He has promised, Himself. He has given us comfort in our darkest hour. He has been right there next to us in every desperate moment. He has given us the assurance that we will one day be united with our daughter for all eternity and this heartache will be no more. He has given us a faith that can say God is still good. He is who He says He is. Job 1:21 says, "The Lord gives and the Lord takes away. Blessed be the name of the Lord."

We know Emma was created for a purpose. We were chosen to be her parents, blessed to love her, and to tell her story. I would not trade the heartbreak or the suffering for a single second. Through this suffering I have received the joy of getting to be the mama of my long, lanky lady and I have had the privilege of knowing Jesus in a way I have never experienced before. Just as her name means "to be made whole", she is made new in the presence of her gracious Father who loves her even more than I. And as for us, we choose to trust the One who knows all, is above all, and is still the same God as when all felt right in our life.

CHAPTER NINE

- EMBRACING -

"Grief knits two hearts in closer bonds than happiness ever can; and common sufferings are far stronger links than common joys."

- Alphonse de Lamartine

On the morning of our wedding in 2005, I was incredibly nervous - sweating, pacing, skittish about probable failure at every turn of the procession we'd rehearsed the day before. I sometimes wonder if these small details were not really the source of my anxiety. I wonder if it was something layered underneath; an internal magnet pulling my gut intuitions out of the here and now and into the future. A current charged with all Julia and I were going to experience in the years ahead running briefly through my body. But I did not think it that day, because later, as soft music hovered over loved ones waiting breathless, as my bride drifted toward me in shining white with pure tears falling only so they might play a part in her radiance, the pull of that internal magnet dissolved - the future was irrelevant, the present paramount. It was the incandescent now that defined us. All who witnessed this felt freedom, then, to build their own daydreams of how our upcoming happiness would surely grow and take form.

But five years later, our now was no longer glorious. Not a soul was constructing daydreams for us; they were struggling enough with suppressing the daily nightmares that seemed to piece together by themselves. The magnet inside pulling toward the future had flipped backwards, yanking us toward the past with malice. Those same witnesses were worrying. Worrying because they should be. More common than any question in those initial months of grieving was this: "How are you guys doing?" When people strangle the "you guys" with nervous inflection like that, here's the translation: "Is your marriage falling apart?" I don't judge this invasive or rude for two reasons. One, it is an absolutely necessary concern aimed at a couple who is watching a life they share unravel before them. Two, it is questions like this that can crack the veneers of silence and denial, which make them the most dangerous and therefore the most courageous questions - revealing to you that the asker might just care enough to willingly walk under this weight with you for awhile.

They ask this question because it is obvious that grief can inflict many horrible things on a marriage. It can blow it up outright. It can kill it slowly, deftly, like an undetectable contagion consumed at every meal together. It can drag one of you into the dark alley of loneliness and beat your hope to death with brass knuckles while the other watches from the street, powerless, until their compassion fatigues and heart turns to selfish stone. It can feign relinquishing its hold, allowing your marriage to appear as though the deafening roar of loss has been muted, but it is just morphing from a mass inside that you can't ignore to an extra layer of worn skin that you won't acknowledge. It can raise one partner out of ashes, only to wound the other further because they're angry, jealous, and depressed that they're still choking on the dust.

However, grief can also join two hearts in an astonishing way that is impossible without the tragedy occurring. It can take two failing hearts and give them one beat, strong enough to pump life through both bodies. But like so many other aspects of grief, it entails that often brutal process of daily letting go of what you desperately desire while daily choosing to take hold of what you desperately need. For Julia and I, losing Emma was the most unyielding threat our marriage has ever faced. However, it has ultimately been the catalyst for a marriage defined by depth, vitality, and more beauty than I knew could exist between two human beings.

The marriage marked by tragedy is a home you build together. The storms that beat down are relentless -

doubt, despondency, selfishness, indifference, and bitterness creep in the back door to escape the rain. And once they're in, they huddle together, seeking to suck the warmth from the fireplace. What do they want more than anything? They want silence. Cold, dead silence. But to kick them out, to fill the house with the loud heat of hopes and dreams and redemption, Julia and I had to be willing to embrace some very distinct ideas.

Embracing Helplessness

Julia and I love Christmas - we love caroling, candy canes, movies, glog, fireplaces flaunting rows of stockings, our sleepy-eyed families in circles unwrapping presents, candle-lit Christmas-Eve services, new pajamas with cartoon reindeer on them, and most of all, the kinetic energy of the Christmas spirit, the anticipation and satisfaction and unity of it all. But the holiday season of 2010 premiered with a whimper for us. The grandeur of Christmas was struck down in its prime. With each commercial showcasing cheerful families in fluffy red sweaters reveling in their abundance, the anticipation of a Christmas morning with our dissevered little family atrophied. With each loving mother we passed on the street, as they cradled newborns in Santa onesies, the dissatisfaction brought on by our unused baby outfits, our empty arms, compounded. With each friend and loved one packing up, cruising off to homes decked with boughs of holly, back to their safe, inclusive Christmas, the harmony of the season disbanded, and we felt defected to that sad lot of long-faced people you see eating Christmas dinner at a seedy Chinese restaurant.

We decided to travel up to Portland. Julia's sister Kaitlyn had recently moved there, and we thought her new apartment would be a more palatable place to gather, if only because the other locations - our home, our parents' homes - would be laden with land mines that discharge all the dreams not realized. To inhabit the empty spaces that were to be filled by Emma seemed an unnecessary holiday purgatory. In some ways, Christmas was the last great bastion of our pre-made imaginations of what life would be like with our daughter. Even back in August, Julia had fashioned her favorite Christmas characteristics with the added freshness and fun of her child on the way - all in razor-sharp detail, all with reckless certainty. This is yet another awful aspect of grief, that as you recede from the initial calamity, you continually discover, as though you had forgotten, that there are more dreams to lay on the altar of loss, more memories you thought you'd have that you must drop down the darkest wells inside you. For they do not leave - like the delusions of even the most medicated schizophrenic, they're always there, waiting for the opportunity at which their leverage might wobble and wound you.

Despite the potential of a harmless city that did not know our past, Christmas was nevertheless one of the emptiest days of our lives. Julia's family tried desperately to distract us, to comfort us, to support us, but they were empty inside too, and hollow people cannot hold each other up. We sat in that apartment and wept. Julia cried harder than ever before. It was as though some invisible fist was wrenching the tears up from her core, racking her body violently with each retrieval, damaging her insides. I held her. I held her for so long. But the tears would not subside. Usually I could whisper a loving word, an encouraging verse from scripture, a practical explanation or even a joke; then the crying would end, the throbs would stop. But not on this day where so many dreams were stolen. In these circumstances, my anger rises. Fine, I can try to lament my own pain without animosity, but when I see Julia hurting like hell, I get angry. I get angry, ultimately, because I'm helpless. I am completely and utterly helpless to stop it; helpless to soothe her or strengthen her or save her.

But wait, what about our culture of self-help? Can't it save us? Our bookstore shelves packed with pages and pages of steps and systems and white-knuckle self-improvement that promise final victory over powerlessness? It is all a ruthless joke. It is the helplessness of self-help - to believe in it, we must run in circles, ignore the ruse, pretend our last attempt at self-reliance didn't really blow up in our faces, then delude ourselves that the next program, the catchier title, the bolder promise on the brighter cover will work to wipe away this constant feeling of falling. It is a tiring exercise in futility. And I knew it. I was helpless to help myself or help Julia. She too was helpless to help herself or help me.

But something happened that day as I was cradling her. Instead of running from it, instead of hating it, I embraced helplessness. I did not speak. I did not piece together what I thought would be the most effective prescription of encouragement for Julia. I gave up fixing, and gave in to incompetence. I gave up trying to carry the load of loss and gave in to my incapability to carry anything. What does this mean? It means I prayed to God on her behalf. That is it. No other thoughts, no other arguments, no other measures. For the first time that Christmas morning, I prayed the prayer I would continue to offer to the Lord every time Julia was cast down by affliction. I would simply hold her tighter and ask over and over again for God to shower her with his Holy Spirit. To comfort her. I must have lifted these requests a hundred times, every time, to God, and with each repetition, I felt the pressure of our mutual need lifting from the muscles in my shoulders, I felt the confidence that comes from coming to the end of ourselves where God waits with all might and power, felt absolutely for the first time what I already knew - that no matter what, Julia is watched over, guarded, protected, and nurtured toward wholeness by her loving God. And here is the crazy thing: it works. With all sincerity and honesty, I can tell you that since that Christmas morning, there has been a multitude of moments where I have repeated the cadence of this prayer, and the cloud oppressing Julia has lifted. And every time it feels like a miracle. It feels like I serve an amazing, astounding, and expansive God who loves me so dearly and so intimately. It feels like my prayers are not ignored or simply heard, but instead answered. It savors of security, for if I can actually embrace the helplessness I so often feel and still love and cherish and serve and support my wife the way I desperately desire to, then it means we can make it through this. And in the end, I rejoice in this fact: If I embrace helplessness, I embrace God.

Embracing Grace

Julia returned to work in January. As we idled at the light, waiting to pull in the hospital entrance, as Julia battled corrupt butterflies poaching on her insides, I seriously considered disregarding the turn, gunning it straight to the freeway, then to the airport, then to a distant land where our world starts over - a place where hospitals exist without hallways haunted by the ghosts of our waking nightmare, without sterile rooms still holding the echoes of our wailing in their walls. Dropping her off at the curb felt like total abandonment. She was strong, no doubt. And she knew that one more week in our empty house might lead to an "all work and no play makes jack a dull boy" situation. Grief paralyzes and props up four walls that continually close in - eventually you must escape if you wish to avoid being snuffed out. Julia felt this when she decided to return to the maternity unit. But just because you're escaping doesn't mean the place you're running to is any more appealing. Especially if it's the exact location where everything fell apart. I watched her walk into the doors, praying that God would strengthen each step, cover each conversation, and display his love through the co-workers that cared so faithfully for her.

Day after day, week after week, the routine took shape. The morning drop-off lessened in its nerves and fear and foreboding. However, the night-time pick-up and drive home were infinitely different. Different because we held a day's worth of recollections and daydreams and disappointments and tiny heartbreaks in our laps. In the morning, that space between driver and passenger was airy, unused. But at night, it was packed, impudent, unavoidable. From the outside in, it would appear that our conversation looked almost identical every time we took this night time drive. For Julia, the formula looks something like this: An ignorant or insensitive comment from an unloving patient disinterested with her new child + a reminder of injustice and unfairness + a look of shallow pity from a doctor + walking past that room in the corner where we wept for three days + stopping a second too long at the nursery window to picture Emma squirming under a heating lamp + seeing a dad cry tears of happiness holding his new baby girl + the sun going down + holding a newborn who looks like her daughter + feeling the emptiness of an empty womb + hating that she has so much love still to give + seeing my tired face force a smile from the driver's side as I pick her up = unload it all before her heart bursts all over the dash. For me, the formula looked something like this: Silence at my desk before anyone else shows up + imagining Emma screaming "Daddy!" when I come home + a passage from literature about a mother whose child dies + seeing Emma as a high school student and marveling at how smart she would be + seeing a co-worker's pictures of his daughter hung proudly + a reminder of injustice and unfairness + lamenting Julia's formula + wondering if my capacity to dream is permanently deformed + hating words because they make sharp what I want to stay dull + seeing Julia's tired face force a smile from the passenger side as I pick her up = catch everything she unloads before her heart bursts all over the dash, then see how much of my own formula I can swallow without being poisoned to death.

From the outside in, it would appear ridiculous just how many times we had these conversations. Almost obnoxious how similar they all sound. But this is where grace must enter. Because honestly, there are many times in grief when the very last thing you want to hear is how your spouse is hurting. In fact, you feel a strange mix of irritation and outrage, not so much with your spouse directly, but with the fact that your spouse has decided to make known yet again the despair that has already been known then re-known then known some more. Their insistence on rehashing the hurt is almost selfish to you, a narcissistic inwardness that does no good - if you could both just lock your sights on a future without hurt, car rides and Sunday walks and family dinners would be much less daunting. But grief just can't operate that way. Grief must be ingested fully then regurgitated completely. To only retain it is to only return to darkness, to desolation. Instead, grace must enter in. Grace allows you to listen to what onlookers would deem the same awful sentiments needlessly repeated over and over, and hear them as unique, worthy of affirmation, and absolutely legitimate. It allows you to understand and appreciate and speak words of comfort to the small, scared, scarred place inside that these words originate from. Grace allows you to stop and listen before trying to mend and fix. It allows you to hear even the most ridiculous, the most erroneous, the most sacrilegious notions streaming from your spouse's lips without needing to immediately correct and control. It allows you to acknowledge the formula of grief bubbling inside you so that you might confirm their pain instead of dismissing it.

Julia gave me grace when I said there is only a barren hush blanketing the universe. I gave her grace when she said God is punishing us. She gave me grace when I said we are destined for only two things: waiting and suffering. I gave her grace when she said she can't do this anymore, can't live life this way, can't take any more steps without falling down forever. Is it tiring, to exchange grace in this way? Unbelievably. But while extending grace is exhausting, it is also exhilarating, because it invites you to display the character of God to the one person you so desperately wish would feel his presence. And I can attest that when I reflect on the grace Julia has shown to me, despite the eclipse of my bold words of sorrow; each time she patiently listened, hugged me, and spoke words of reconciling love, I felt that maybe, just maybe, our world could be well again. So as we sat in the car driving home, as Julia once again relinquished the burden she had accumulated that day, I offered only grace. But this is not a paltry gift - for if by giving grace we allow the ones we love to trust us enough to empty themselves before the night falls, we prepare a small space for a loving God to claim when the sun rises.

Embracing Transparency to Others

By the time you've withstood your hundredth insensitive or ignorant or oddly manipulative response from an outsider regarding your hardship, you are dreaming of ways to grieve it in a vacuum. By the time you feel for the hundredth time like a sideline spectator stuck watching the fast-paced game of normal life everyone else gets to gleefully play in, you are ruminating about ways to hide beneath the bleachers before anyone notices. By the time you've considered for the hundredth time how a married pair passing by you is carrying your dream like a picnic basket, swinging it to and fro with easy smiles from easy journeys, you want to move into a cottage behind a massive mountain in a sparsely populated country whose few people are known for being uninviting and unobtrusive.

But we wanted to feel normal, to feel like we could co-exist with non-grievers; perhaps their joviality was like a communicable disease we could catch if only by breathing it in once in a while. Wouldn't it feel good to be 'that couple' instead of 'that couple that lost their baby'? Julia and I were faced every day with the often disarming choice of whether or not we'd tell our saga of woe to those we met. So often, we settled for dishonest small talk: "How was your week?" Truthful response: Like diving into an abyss of anguish with a boiling pool of misery at the bottom, you? Actual response: "Good, good. How about you?" Then, "What did you guys do this weekend?" Truthful response: Exactly what we did the last 10 weekends. Woke up, cried before leaving the bed, went to a farmer's market crawling with mothers and fathers and babies tucked in the very same front pack we were forced to shove into storage, then to a movie starring characters that see their dreams come true, then back to bed where we cried before falling asleep. Actual response: "It was good, yours?" And this is how the exercise in dodging hidden truth can play out, week after week. Why the lack of transparency? Because there are so many benefits of autonomous grieving:

1. <u>You are a conversational and relational martyr</u>.

The basic thought is this - this new acquaintance who is smiling in front of me, talking about important sports or important food or important jobs that involve wearing a tie does not deserve to be slapped in the face with my difficulty. It would be so cruel, even sadistic, to ram this conversation into the brick wall of my distressing realities. Therefore, as the withholder of truth, I am actually selfless. I am sparing another human being even the smallest share in my suffering. I am saving them from a hard conversation on their car-ride home or a rogue tear they never intended to shed. This is my affliction. No need to spread it.

2. You can retain the pride you have left because no one will have the opportunity to pity you.

The misconception is that when something like this happens, all pride is inevitably stripped from you, that you become this fountain of transparency - all who search for total truth can swim in it, because you've lost all and therefore you keep nothing. Unfortunately, I seem to have a bottomless reservoir of pride. Part of me hates when people tilt their head to the side, let their mouths droop into awkward lip pouts they rarely practice, place a limp noodle hand on my hardened shoulder, and say (translated) "I pity you." Part of me wants to dig back, burrow underneath their skin, beneath the rugs where their secrets have been swept, and find a way to pity them, because that will make me feel like we're even. Because as strange as it sounds, after intense loss, when everything seems out of control and unjust, it is enticing to snatch control back by evening the scales between myself and my fellow man - we may not share this difficulty, but I see you, and you deserve pity too, my friend. And if you would simply understand that, the creepy half-frown on your face just might vanish.

3. You don't have to name it and therefore relive it.

This, I think, is the greatest benefit of refusing to tell your true story. Because it is impossible to explain what you've been going through without re-dressing yourself with that mourning garb, without being attacked by moving images of your living nightmare. The tale cannot be explained quickly either, because that would liken betrayal - to hurry through some minimized, Cliff's Notes version of a loss so deep, of someone so loved, seems cold-hearted. So you do the opposite. You say nothing. This allows you to stay in the present while the gaping mouth of the not-so-distant past is restrained from consuming you. In your secretive silence, you are awarded the right to deal in shallow, breezy conversations like everyone else, and this, oddly, makes you feel normal again. You get so you crave this normalcy like a drug. You get so you desire to tread water up at the surface where the rest of the world takes strong breathes of ocean air, to wink and wave like you belong there; instead of being forced yet again to grab someone's hand and drag them to the true depths you've been swimming in for what feels like endless days. And this is how you slowly, methodically transition from the always accurate inclination that "not everyone needs to know" to the always exiling justification that "no one needs to know."

4. No one can tell you difficult truths you don't want to hear.

In some ways, I believe this is a benefit for anyone who wants to simultaneously exist in and out of community. They are in community because they share space and laughs and drinks and recipes with other human beings, but out of community because they refuse to share anything that intrudes on their privacy, or in other words, would cause them to consider changing. For Julia and I, this was heightened, intensified. Because I deemed myself afflicted, I also wanted to deem myself untouchable. It seems rational - why would I tell anyone about something that they could never possibly speak into? They'll only fumble and fuddle around with a response they've never had nor wanted to deliver before, make me feel more like a stranger at someone else's Thanksgiving dinner, make me feel like I should be moving on, make me listen to the trials of their cousin and his wife that they say is just like ours but stopped being like ours the moment they started speaking, make me feel more inclined to get another drink and fill it to the brim. But it's fear, really. I am terrified that if someone were to know me peeled of all the layers of prepared answers, prepared assurances, prepared scriptures, and prepared prayers, they might actually point to something I'm unprepared to acknowledge. They might challenge me, throw out an affront to my incorrect thoughts, my claim to self-pity, my inner-declarations about this independent suffering I'm enduring. So if I keep them in the dark, keep their questions and advice and wisdom at the margins, I retain the sickly satisfying right to plant my feet and never take a step in any direction that scares me.

~

There is a scene at the end of the film *Into the Wild* that I will never be able to shake. Chris, the main character, had disappeared from his previous life and spent years trekking the country like a solo nomad. Along the way, he makes momentary connections with a host of interesting and loving people while his guilty and grief-stricken parents wait by the phone. In this last scene, he is about to die alone in an abandoned bus in the Alaskan wilderness after ingesting toxic seeds. At one point in the film he tells Ron, a gentle, elderly widower who offers to be his legal guardian, that "you're wrong if you think the joy of life comes principally from human relationships." So he continues his solitary search for self, for a discovery of purpose outside populations. But here at the end, wasted away to 75 pounds, starving to death with no one by his side, he scrawls with shaking fingers this final thought, "HAPPINESS ONLY REAL WHEN SHARED." And as he descends upon his final breath, he pulls a warm coat over his racked body and his marred mind slips into one sun-lit and sparkling hallucination: There is a house. His family rushes out of the front door. And Chris is there to greet them. He has returned home safely. They are hugging and they are weeping and they are rejoicing in redemption for all that has been lost. But alas, it is not real.

In so many ways, this gets to the core of why it feels so dissatisfying to allow grief to separate you from community. Julia and I can think we are protecting ourselves; escaping the pain that only other humans, with their words like knives, can inflict. We think that maybe one day what has died inside of us might spring back to life if only given its own parcel of land planted far from brotherhood, a space to let its vulnerable seed take root. Our own bus in the wilderness. But this is like constructing a false cocoon with only a first act. It begins sturdy. It is protective. It feels like safety. But in reality it entraps, it isolates, it barricades the world outside, and there is no redeeming epilogue; no real butterfly beauty is ultimately produced. We, like Chris, would be left creating our own fading daydreams of hugs and tears and the act of reclaiming relationships lost or stolen or deepening those yet to be discovered. But alas, they would not be real. We would be alone and dying slowly.

~

What is beautiful is not just when happiness is shared, but sadness also. This is also real. Maybe more real. Maybe sharing our grief is the closest we can ever possibly get to being communally human. And perhaps that is why community in the midst of suffering has been one of the greatest blessings Julia and I have received in our lifetimes. We love it when the realization hits that we are not just two bodies in a room with other bodies, that our conversations are not defined by that which is fleeting but by that which lasts, which matter; that we are loved, cared for, and challenged. We love it when, though it can be awkward and messy, we truly feel like our lives are not removed from these other lives, that they share our heart and we share theirs. So we are not conversational martyrs, because we know that when we try to convince ourselves that we are falling on our swords to spare others' feelings, we are in actuality waving the blade to hold others at bay, and we are missing out on accepting their flesh and blood and heart and hands as our armor against the next wave of attacks from our worst enemy - hopelessness. We dispense of pride; our marriage does not have to appear perfect, appear stable, or appear particularly godly. It must only appear. And we need not claw at others, tearing them down, so that we might hitch ourselves up a ladder we think is leading to self-reliance but ultimately ends at the busy and blighting intersection of bitterness and dejection. We accept that we need people, and we let what feels at first like pity from others purify itself, transfigure into compassion. This compassion hems into the very fabric of our souls - it takes time, takes a heart ripped open, but this tapestry of empathy is always sublime, and saves like eternal stitches sewn deep until we finally see heaven. And yes, we must relive it. We must give the darkness words again and again and again. But an odd thing happens once you've given your disfigured story to other people, let them hold it in their own palms, let them possess it, let them study it later with all its withered scope and weakened substance. You realize that they will not keep it as collateral against you, or as a reminder that their life is better than yours. They keep it as a keepsake that resounds with the pulse of new connectivity - a sign that they are not the only ones who suffer, that vulnerability is possible, that condolence is necessary. They consider, perhaps for the first time, the frightening yet freeing possibility of purging the back pocket in their own heart where all the tortured memories and shelved dreams and hopes dashed are heaped together like starving children in a lightless mine shaft. They see you, with all your bruises and cracked bones, and they do not see a pitiable being, but instead they see themselves, and the second this occurs, God is able to pour mercy like rain on the parched plains between you. This, I believe, is how God intended his creation to co-exist. And now that there is a healthy, flourishing garden of mutual grace between you, hard truths proposed to you lose their edge, lose their judgment, and sing only of service and sanctification.

~

I am certain that God intended to use community as his most profound instrument of comfort. We bare witness to this - Christ showed himself so abundantly through the words and actions of our friends and family, and he is still displaying himself through all of them in incredible ways. I am reminded of a moving exchange from *The Brothers Karamazov* by Fyodor Dostoyevsky in which a reverenced elder monk is speaking to a woman who, by her own account, is vexed by "a lack of faith."

The woman says: "I say to myself, 'What if I've been believing all my life, and when I come to die there's nothing but the burdocks growing on my grave?' How – how can I get back my faith? How can I prove it?" And the monk responds: "There's no proving it, though you can be convinced of it." She says: "How?" And the monk responds with this: "By the experience of active love. Strive to love your neighbor actively and constantly. In so far as you advance in love you will grow surer of the reality of God and of the immortality of your soul. If you attain perfect self-forgetfulness in the love of your neighbor, then you will believe without doubt. This has been tried. This is certain."[6]

[6] Dostoyevsky, Fyodor. *The Brothers Karamazov*. Simon & Brown. 2011.

This has been tried in our lives - we have received active love by those we are in community with. It has saved our lives. The selflessness of others has made Julia and I all the more certain that Christ loves us, and that, despite any and all circumstances, he is completely for us.

Embracing Hope

Months passed. Days were not days as they had been before tragedy. They dragged longer and yet felt fractured. Mornings were quiet, tasted of cold, a drafty peacefulness - the aroma of coffee a loyal friend that hadn't changed. Open scripture, let time stand still, let God speak, let him know this hour is not enough, this world is not enough, this veil between us makes me worse than blind. Then the work day; my mind flips a switch, curtains rise and the play begins, I am in so many ways an actor, and my body calls for reinforcement - millions of microscopic workers donning yellow hard hats jump to attention, start constructing each smile for me, pulley up each interested eye brow; a thousand tiny hands massage my vocal chords so my speech strikes strong and my laugh rings true. They pour concrete into my tear ducts, let it dry, and pray it holds. Inside me, the minions are running in all directions, screaming orders at each other, focused because they have to be, like they're operating a trauma unit that just overflowed with earthquake victims. They're patching and stitching, staunching and soothing, building a scaffold for all that is cracking and crumbling.

Somewhere near my heart there is a miniscule foreman posted, watching with wide eyes, considering closing up shop to let it all bleed out. He's wondering, "Will we get a break today?" Yes, a few; there are real smiles, real laughter, real brotherhood with those I call friend, real waves of love and encouragement washing over. My drive home when Julia is not working - silence like the morning but with a darker hue, like the silence that sits next to a child on a front stoop after his dad never showed up. I'm home. Julia is making a dinner she hopes smells of comfort and tastes like belonging. A kiss and a long hug - the cue for my microscopic workers to clock out, get some hard-earned sleep. The concrete they poured cracks; tears of exhaustion mostly, but occasionally they are tears of missing, of hating that hopelessness recruits Julia's heart, of weathering a slide-show of That Day, my daughter's face, her stolen future. Then, perhaps, a sweet reprieve, an hour of fellowship, an inappropriate joke that springs forth a shade of laughter we thought we'd lost. On the best nights, a clear picture of a sufficient God, a cheer of redemption, a prayer of gratitude, then a tranquil sleep without nightmares.

~

We had started driving up to Reality in Ventura every Sunday to sit under the teaching of Britt Merrick. We wept through the service most weeks - always tears of sadness for loss mixed with tears of thankfulness for

Christ's love. Had it been our choice, church would have met seven days a week. The sermon series Britt began the week we started attending was through the book of Philippians, with the focus of having joy in the midst of suffering. Not a coincidence. His explication of this scripture was so bold, so brave, and so encouraging. It sliced through all the false notions we had agreed upon in our hearts throughout the week, replaced them with grace and truth, and nurtured us toward a fuller appreciation for God. I will never be able to explain my gratitude for these first six months at Reality - never in my life had I felt in a church building the Holy Spirit so palpably, the love of Christ so personally, the might of God so radically.

But that was Sunday. Monday through Saturday was different. We had entered a new and difficult phase. If grief is a dinner party (granted, the worst of all dinner parties), we had entered that phase where the leftover laughter from the last guests stepping out your door has dissipated; when the house falls library quiet, when the energy that filled the space evaporates, when the mess that's left seems to multiply before your eyes, and you feel that gnawing pit in your stomach that says, "All that comfort of brotherhood was a fiction. Now you must face yourself. Now you will know complete loneliness." More and more months into grieving, the daily calls weren't coming. The encouraging texts were less frequent. The cards, and flowers, and family members staying with us were no more. And the fear and anxiety you feel at this is not tied to a disappointment with those people - you understand that inevitably their intentional support must with time pass on - the fear is tied instead to a realization that you will now be forced to take in a closer view of the difficulties you're experiencing. Family and friends had buffered this view; they allowed us to remain fixed on the time line we did not desire to move forward. Their calls affirmed that it was okay to be grieving. Their texts confirmed that we were still in need of help. Their flowers attested to the worth of Emma's life, their cards to the worth of ours, and their company to the belief that we could make it through the day. But now, Julia and I sat across from one another on a couch in what felt like the emptiest house ever built, and the only thing joining us was the unwelcome and unhinging recognition that we would, in fact, have to keep living our lives. We named all of this to one another. We named it because it was safe here in the space between us. Out in the wide open world, where the masses of people marched on with their lives, every conversation with a stranger was a grenade that's pin gets removed at the turn of a question: Do you have children? Even more difficult, perhaps, were the interactions with certain friends and family. Though they cared, Julia and I could not remain protected, because inevitably the despondency they leased on our behalf would spill like sour milk into the space between us. We refused to name that, for the only thing worse than the sting of being pitied is the sting of being ignored. But when Julia and I were alone together, we were shielded - it was a leaky shack, threatening not to hold through winter, but a shelter nonetheless. We named it all because we knew how to. We'd done it before. And though I hated to admit it, I realized there existed God's fingerprints in this. A hint that perhaps we had been, in some significant way, prepared for this. Ridiculous. But the facts illuminate. Scarred by waiting through infertility. Feeling alone. Then naming it. Seeking God and finding him. Lead to a better path, his path. Could perspective materialize? Could a future be waiting after all this waiting? Could healing come here as it had come to us before? My heart said maybe. My mind said absolutely not. Grief is really a very stunted lens to look through - it only offers two subjects: barbed clarity of the damaged past and a skewed, hazy aspect of the present. It can not look to the future; when it tries, all it can produce is a foreshadowing of the currency it deals in - death, destruction, and dire forebodings. There are no longer routine trips to the store - there are only those you love stepping with fragile bones into fragile cars waiting to be struck, to be destroyed, to be maimed and killed in an instant. There are no longer communication mix ups. When you can't get ahold of your sister, your brother, your mother, there is only kidnapping, murder, or accidental death. Your psyche is invaded by these terrible thoughts, these burglars, who it seems have waited for your innocence to be severed, for you to see behind the curtain at the worst of life on earth, so they might slither in, color your imagination black, and never leave. So thus, another choice. If Julia and I were to face the future, to step toward the frightening prospect of newness, we would have to choose to ally ourselves with the last remaining menace: hope.

~

In one of my favorite films, *The Shawshank Redemption*, there is a scene in which Red, a seasoned veteran of Shawshank prison, is educating Andy on the necessary mindset to have while incarcerated. He says, "Hope? Let me tell you something, my friend. Hope is a dangerous thing. Hope can drive a man insane. It's got no place on the inside. You'd better get used to that idea."

Our bout with grief was, at times, much like a prison. The physical is simply replaced by the mental, the emotional. Walls erected by the memories that haunt you, the questions that feel unanswered, the fears that isolate you. Bars fashioned by dreams lost and plans disintegrated. And oddly enough, it was at this phase, further removed from the initial calamity, that hope became a scarier and scarier proposition. It makes far more sense to temper hope, to subdue and dismiss it, to protect yourself from the inevitable defeats and disappointments life brings; because after all, when things have gone so badly, when all that should be complete is grossly abridged, it certainly feels like hope truly does have no use here, and that, at the end of the day, you'd better get used to that idea.

But God meets us in that prison cell, and the closer I drew near to him, the more I was convinced that he intends and even desires for us to have a hope that is dangerous. A hope that defies logic. A hope that stands in the face of years of difficulties and even appears, to some, like it is foolish given the situation. But to have a tempered, guarded hope is to believe in a limited, small god. Because our God transcends doubt. He is a gracious savior, a blessed comforter who has given us himself, the greatest treasure on earth and in heaven. Julia and I spoke these things to one another. Our marriage had been marked by suffering, and there was life-giving intimacy between us through that shared hardship, but our partnership was now sketched with something even more breathtaking: a shared hope in Christ, no matter the circumstances. My soul-mate and I, sitting on a couch, closer than we'd ever been, choosing to believe that the sun would show up again. And it felt so right, so contenting. It was a decision, above all, to refuse the enemy's offer to pitch our tent in the desert and camp out, but to instead continue walking. Though there appeared ahead of us only miles of sand, days of walking without water, months of burning under the brutal heat of life without Emma, we would, by God's grace, put one foot in front of the other, preaching the soothing breeze of faith to each other until all the redemption and joy yet unseen was revealed in all its glory.

Romans 5:3-5 says, "We exalt in our tribulations, knowing that tribulation brings about perseverance; and perseverance, proven character; and proven character, hope; and hope does not disappoint, because the love of

God has been poured out within our hearts through the Holy Spirit who was given to us." Julia and I chose to believe that hope in our God does not disappoint, and we proclaimed, as it says in Hebrews, that we "hold tightly without wavering to the hope we profess, for God can be trusted to keep his promise." There is freedom in a dangerous hope. There is joy in a dangerous faith. And it was through this understanding that we came to hope in the plan of a Heavenly Father that, "through his mighty power at work within us, is able to accomplish infinitely more than we might ask or imagine."

~

Eight months had passed and April came. With it, a reassured outlook on the future despite the peril of our status quo. The reward of witnessing the strengthened faith, challenged hearts, and changed lives of those who had watched us walk through all of this thanks to the grace of God. The joy of a marriage that swims in deepest waters. Sadness and tears still a daily dose, but labeled appropriately, digested authentically, and surrendered deliberately. Peace from knowing Christ as supreme and feeling his infinite love. Rest for our weary souls.

It is possible that as you read this, you're subconsciously attributing our contentment to a passage of time. As the saying goes, "time heals all wounds." There is not a more careless lie, a more damaging promise to a person wading through grief. It is so faulty -

wounds do not heal. Not on this side of heaven. No, you might say, these wounds, with time, will close up. Of course, scars will remain, but even scars fade, melt into the tone of our skin until they are nearly invisible to the naked eye. And your evidence is less tears, more steps forward, more replacements of what's been lost. You would say, "See, they had more children. They got remarried. Found a new boyfriend. They have a nicer step-parent. They got a new job. A new dog. They laugh at romantic comedies again. They don't look down at the carpet so much at Christmas. They plan more trips, more parties, more happy memories. And most of all, they don't talk about what they lost anymore." But wounds are only healed into scars if they no longer bleed. And the wounds from tragedy, from heartache; they bleed. Always, always they bleed.

There is a couple in my parents' small group; a lovely, gracious, loving couple who have been happily married for over forty years. They've had children, they've had successes, they've had a vibrant relationship with Christ - it appears obvious that whatever difficulties they could have experienced, time must have healed them, because they're so content. But on a night when my parents broke down before them, sharing the loss of their granddaughter Emma, a backstory emerged from this couple, escaped before their lips could catch it. One that nobody knew. They too had lost their first born child. It was sudden, unexpected, horrific, tragic. They wept aged tears dug up from the murkiest reservoirs inside them. The wound was bleeding here in a crowded living room with people who were not there when it was first inflicted. Forty years. And there it was, ready to surface. Ready to flow forth in tedious gushes. Do you not feel them, your own wounds? Do they not bleed when you hear a certain song, inhale a certain scent, see a certain person, place, or thing? Do they not bleed when a vision, a memory, or a dream deferred blind-sides you in the aisle of a grocery store, in the seat of your car, in the bunker of your own bedroom? Has time really healed them? If anything, time is the isolator, pressuring you daily, expecting you to do anything but rightly regard your pain. It wants you to look around, see the seasons changing, and act accordingly. Though your heart exists in Winter, time forces Spring upon it, and you are severed from others in the strangest way - they see the sun shining on your once broken heart and await it's healthy beat, and yet you know yours is a December heart that will not, can not thaw.

But in my experience, it is not time that heals all wounds. It is Christ who thaws the core of frozen hearts, of men and women bleeding to death from gaping wounds. Yes, we bleed because that's what human beings do. We are dying. Paul says in 2 Corinthians 1, "We were crushed and completely overwhelmed, and we thought we would never live through it. In fact, we expected to die. But as a result, we learned not to rely on ourselves, but on God who can raise the dead. And he did deliver us...we are confident that he will continue to deliver us...he will rescue us." We are bleeding recklessly and yet new blood is transfused by his grace. We are weakened daily and yet we are strong eternally. We are captured by loss and yet rescued by his love. We are dying and yet we are raised to life. All in Christ, always.

CHAPTER TEN

- BELIEVING -

"Man shall begin by loving the unseen, God, for thereby he himself shall learn what it is to love. But the fact that he really loves the unseen shall be indicated precisely by this, that he loves the brother he sees. The more he loves the unseen, the more he will love the men he sees."

- Soren Kierkegaard

It was in a discussion with my students that I knew my heart had stepped over a new border, entered a new domain. We were reading a speech by Albert Camus entitled "The Unbeliever and Christians." In it, Camus, a professed atheist, is speaking to an audience of professed Christians: "The world of today needs Christians who remain Christians...What the world expects of Christians is that Christians should speak out, loud and clear, and that they should voice their condemnation in such a way that never a doubt, never the slightest doubt, could rise in the heart of the simplest man. That they should get away from abstraction and confront the blood-stained face history has taken on today. The grouping we need is a grouping of men resolved to speak out clearly and to pay up personally...Perhaps we cannot prevent this world from being a world in which children are tortured. But we can reduce the number of tortured children. And if you don't help us, who else in the world can help us do this? And what I know - which sometimes creates a deep longing in me - is that if Christians made up their minds to it, millions of voices - millions, I say - throughout the world would be added to the appeal of a handful of isolated individuals who, without any sort of affiliation, today intercede almost everywhere and ceaselessly for children and for men."[7] I listened to my students as they wrestled with the text and with each other, ultimately agreeing with Camus on a sincere and integral front - that what the world needs is followers of Christ who walk like Christ, who speak up and defend and rescue and love like Christ, who are in fact Christians. I did not feel the temptation to provide an additional caveat, a more palatable explication, a less confrontational take on confrontational truths. I kept looking at his final thoughts, the words he used - intercede...ceaselessly. To intercede: acting on behalf of one who is in trouble. Ceaselessly: always.

[7] Camus, Albert. "The Unbeliever and Christians." 1948.

We had suffered and we were comforted. We had lived in forlorn trouble, and there were those who interceded ceaselessly on our behalf. There were those calling themselves Christians who had remained Christians. Now, forged inside me was an explicit desire to comfort others in the same way. 2 Corinthians 1: 3-4 says; "All praise to the God and Father of our Lord Jesus Christ. He is the source of every mercy and the God who comforts us. He comforts us in all our troubles so that we can comfort others. When others are troubled, we will be able to give them the same comfort God has given us." I am rushed back to the burning house, where those who burned beside me testify that Jesus Christ is alive and consoling, where God displayed his active love for me through others, where I am transformed. I wanted now more than anything to spend the rest of my life being one who dives into the flames, pulls the chair across the charred room, places it leg to leg with the suffering seat, and endures the burn in solidarity; that at that moment when he who hurts lifts his leaden head and downcast eyes to mine, the gaze of a comforting Christ would wash over him. As Julia often put it, "Our hearts for the hurting beat louder."

~

I knew enough to test these desires with scripture. In the windowless chambers of grief, scripture had become the light; often the only source. I came before it with requests: sustain me; teach me; give me a reason to keep stumbling forward, keep breathing, keep believing. I came before it with absolute dependence. With trust that it was literal and absolute, without ambiguity. Trust that it could not be contextualized and commentaried away, that it was bare and bold and beautiful. The Word answered all requests. For sorrow, it was relief. For anger, it was perspective. For anxiety, it was rest. For abandonment, it was adoption. For lies, it was truth. The relationship between the word of God and I had irrevocably altered. Never to return to the surface - always to remain as an interchange of rescuer and rescued. I, the drowned, it, the CPR, of life pumped through, never to return void. And now, eight months after the squall first hit, I was reading other sections of the Bible with that same desperation, with the same willingness to heed the words plainly, without human explanation shoved in between. Verses like Isaiah 58: 6-7, that says, "Free those who are wrongly imprisoned...let the oppressed go free, and remove the chains that bind people. Share your food with the hungry, and give shelter to the homeless. Give clothes to those who need them." Or Proverbs 31: 8-9 which implores us to "Speak up for those who cannot speak for themselves; ensure justice for those being crushed. Yes, speak up for the poor and helpless, and see that they get justice." And Proverbs 28:27, which submits that "Whoever gives to the poor will lack nothing. But a curse will come upon those who close their eyes to poverty." Or 1 John 3: 17-18, which tells me that "If someone has enough money to live well and sees a brother or sister in need but shows no compassion - how can God's love be in that person? Dear children, let's not merely say that we love each other; let us show the truth by our actions." Then James, who aims for the crux of it in these verses from the second chapter: "What good is it, dear brothers and sisters, if you say you have faith but don't show it by your actions? Can that kind of faith save anyone? Suppose you see a brother or sister who has no food or clothing, and you say, 'Good-bye and have a good day; stay warm and eat well' - but then you don't give that person any food or clothing. What good does that do? So you see, faith by itself isn't enough. Unless it produces good deeds, it is dead and useless."

I did not have ears to hear these verses three years before. Guaranteed, the minute I read them, I would have started assembling defenses, formulating explanations, relishing in sensible arguments for why it would not actually be expected of me to serve those who suffer. I would produce a list of sins I don't commit, of other things I do for God that are also in the Bible, that are also what he commands, that are deemed by my church and my parents as Christianly; then I would ball it up, pack it together, and bash it against these scriptures, tell them to go away, to quit lining my mind, heart, and soul like unwelcome spiritual leeches. I would show God that I am a good man, a good husband, a good father; and that family and jobs and security come first and I would search desperately for anyone or anything that would confirm this as true. I would throw my deeds on my home-made morality scale, my acts of Christianity that slip and slither under and around these texts but never through them, until they dissolved into those cloudy spaces inside me where comforting human logic and sweet, sweet denial captures them, chokes them out, and relegates them to this awful destiny: awakened only by courageous stories of other Christians being true Christians in the world, then put to sleep by my own cowardice.

Then that terrible vision would crystallize again in my mind: There is a dark theatre filled with thousands of people, all hopeless, and afflicted, and destined for eternal misery. They're watching my life on a giant screen. It is a silent film; no subtitles. Somehow I know this is the way God wants to reveal himself to each and every one of them. Oh, how he desires it. But only my actions can be seen. The audience cannot hear my interpretations. My clarifications. They cannot hear my friends or family or pastors eloquently enabling my lack of obedience. They cannot hear me philosophize and theorize and publicize my sincere care for hurting people I won't actually help. They only observe whose eyes meet mine, whose hands I hold, whose crying faces I press against my shoulder, who I feed and shelter and free, who I fight for; and who, though my mouth is moving, my body ignores.

This multitude of people packed in the theatre have Bibles in their laps, given license to read it cover to cover between scenes. They've been told by the ticket vendor that they will surely witness something miraculous, beyond all expectations. That what they're about to see is the life of a Christian, and therefore it must be amazing, because all Christians share the same story - each one has been radically loved by God, who sent his only son to die on the cross so that they might have life, and life eternal - inevitably they respond to this abundant love in incredible ways. "Wait and see," the vendor would announce as the people limp in to view my life, "see how this man who has been rescued by a glorious God will give his life away in loving others. Because it's the only legitimate response to such a sacrifice." But alas, when the lights come up and the credits roll, my fears would be confirmed. The spectators found the beauty of a God who cares for the orphans and widows, delivers the oppressed, liberates the slave, and endures rejection and persecution for the good of mankind - they found it in the words they read from the Bible on their lap - but in the end, they discovered only the ugliness of self-preservation in my actions on the screen. And they wonder as they shuffle out if Christ's sacrifice for humanity was really all that big if the life of I who believe in him is so very, very small.

But this had changed. The plot had twisted. The act break in our lives had been dramatic, but the grace of God even more so. Now, as I laid down to sleep at night, I imagined those in the theatre scooting up in their seat just a bit. To see; to really see what God can do with poor, lost sinners who have lost their very hearts. I imagine that as they behold Christ's love for us, as they watch the sunset of anguish pass over and the dawn of hope rise up, as they see us walking upright, worshipping God with our active love for others, they are perceiving a stirring in their own hearts. I imagine they are feeling something that they've never felt before. They are looking down to that book in their lap, they are pouring the words into their own souls, they are smiling at one another, nodding in agreement, pointing with enthusiasm to the film of our lives as proof of its realness. They do not shuffle out in confusion any longer. They stay now. They stay and pray and cry and laugh and dream about their own films, their own possibility to be used as a candle in the corner of the world's darkest rooms. And this new vision brings peace. Brings glory to God. Brings possibilities to be more like Christ to more people who need to touch him, to know him, to love him.

~

With the loss of Emma, the seen world fell away. Before all of this, Julia and I had stood in the Times Square of our lives, awaiting a grand celebration - but the core of the earth shook. The buildings crumbled like kicked-over sand castles, neon bulbs on falling signs popping streams of light that snap in instants to an indifferent blackout, streets splitting into concrete rivers, cars piling one on another. There we were in the center, on a curb, alone.

But when the seen world is erased, the eternal is drawn with sharper lines. And when you see that art, the art of the eternal, displayed in all its soul-shaking glory, you cannot, you must not turn your face away. You must never leave that heavenly gallery where the eternal is revealed. Though our lives had crumbled, Julia and I wanted now more than anything to seek only the eternal; so instead of trying to rebuild the world around us exactly as it had been, instead of remodeling more sand castles that are easily displaced by the next strong tide, we sought to remain in the reality of what is unseen and yet known; to love as Christ loves, leaving our curb and searching for the ones lost amidst the wreckage around us. For is there anything more satisfying than to realize that as you faithfully remain in the gallery of the eternal, seeing its art clearly, loving deeply, you have become yourself, by the grace of the Almighty God, a part of the exhibit?

CHAPTER ELEVEN

- RISKING -

"There is no way to peace along the way of safety. For peace must be dared, it is itself the great venture and can never be safe. Peace is the opposite of security. To demand guarantees is to want to protect oneself. Peace means giving oneself completely to God's commandment."

- Dietrich Bonhoeffer

I was sitting in church and listening to a man on the stage pour out his passion for the least of these in Ventura. I was listening to the stories of brokenness he saw play out there - pregnant teenagers banished and single mothers warring with addiction and single fathers who've spent half their years in prison and schizophrenics haunted by polluted voices from within and runaways with frightened parents scouring the obituaries and old men waving white flags with whiskey as their sole surviving companion and young men and women roaming sleepless weeks from tent to tent willing to kill for meth; all living in a river bottom where drugs and prostitution and rape and murder are a nightly reality. I was listening to the plight of these outcasts, of being relegated to this hellish quarantine beneath a bridge as the unclean, the menaces, the lepers who have infected themselves with sores. It was the chorus of dead dreams. Last gasps of aspiration giving in to the irredeemable sleep of hopelessness.

But I was also listening to the stories of reparation this man encountered through the homeless outreach he'd started - mothers embracing abandoned children, fathers humbly renewing kinship with families they abused, forty years of alcoholism conquered by one day of love, prodigals returning home reconciled, a couple stealing for a fix now giving food for the hungry - all the skeletons thrust out of closets clustered with brittle bones, then burned away by the pure flame of forgiveness. And above all, Jesus Christ glorified.

The Holy Spirit worked me over that day. Planted a seed of calling that would grow into a beautifully unruly conviction whether I watered it with obedience or not. I went home in a stupor - I had left my heart in the church, on the stage, inside and around the possibility of being an active agent of Jesus Christ in Ventura, of pronouncing hope to the hopeless, of raising my voice for the voiceless. But back to work. Back to responsibilities. Back to my routine. Discontent, but the holy kind; the kind that does not devalue or tear down your current environment, but bolsters your desire and vision for something more. A new step of faith. It feels like a first step. A necessary lunge forward because you have encountered the living God. Bonhoeffer says, "The road of faith passes through obedience to the call of Jesus. Unless a definite step is demanded, the call vanishes into thin air, and if men imagine that they can follow Jesus without taking this step, they are deluding themselves like fanatics."[8] I was on the true road of faith now. I knew that. I wanted to look ahead - the road of faith is not straight, not marked with yellow lines, is not even visible. It offers only the pledge of a firm patch of concrete beneath your feet and the promise that your next step will land on solid ground. I desired so badly not to delude myself. I had met my God. My savior. And I did not want this call to vanish into thin air. I wanted it to materialize, to make itself known. Not in bold letters in the sky but in bold movements of my shaky legs, of courage, with willingness to withhold safety for the peace of passionate service for Jesus Christ.

I met with the man on the stage. I told my story and he told his. We dreamed together about the call of Christ, the plight of the poor, the recognition that there is little difference between the loss Julia and I tasted and the loss these men and women and children consume every night on the streets. He had been praying that God would bring workers for the harvest. I had been praying that God would allow us to be a part of that harvest. It was a sweet

---

[8] Bonhoeffer, Dietrich. *The Cost of Discipleship*. Touchstone. 1995.

fellowship. In fact, it was like a long-overdue reunion, and this, I believe, should be the nature of all bonds between brothers and sisters joining in the liberation of lost lives - you can link hands because you have let go of all else; forsaken the world so that you might love those in the world. But back to work. Back to responsibilities. Back to my routine. Discontent, but the holy kind. It was Spring, and I was a couple months away from the end of the school year. Only weeks away from needing to decide whether or not I would commit to another year teaching in Pasadena. Julia and I started praying about moving up to Ventura. About the possibility of me leaving my job and serving without pay at the daily homeless outreach there. About our lives changing in a radical way. Again.

~

It was an interesting time, an often conflicted time. I understood more than ever that the most difficult decisions in life are never a question of good versus bad. They are almost always a question of the good versus the greater. They're the decisions that, soon after you've chosen the one path, you are bombarded with all that the other path has to offer. These considerations and concerns that come rushing into your head are not easily dismissed - they pull at your heart, appeal to your mind, make you question and question and then question some more.

The Good: Avoiding big changes in the midst of grief.

Julia wrote this blog post on her first Mother's Day after losing Emma:

Last May, I had celebrated my first mother's day when I was pregnant; it is etched in my mind forever. I was filled with such joy, such anticipation, and such thanksgiving for the chance to be a mother. To my surprise and pure delight, I received my first mother's day card written from little EJW, but transcribed by her daddy. It brought me to tears - hormone induced, dream fulfilled, alligator tears. I was receiving a card from my baby - it was amazing. We went to breakfast and celebrated the gift that was growing inside me. It was just as I imagined it would be; unobliterated happiness.

A year later everything has changed. My heart feels so heavy - there's a good chance it might just fall out of its rightful place in my chest cavity. This can be a beautiful day celebrated by millions of mothers, but for some it's painful, and for me it brings a wave of sorrow. I had a baby. She never lived outside of me. Yes, I am a mother, but it is not the way it should be. I have never 'mothered' outside of a pregnancy. We have been on the cusp of parenthood for years now, but we've never 'parented.' It is raw and so very painful.

This weekend I will grieve some more. I will allow myself to feel all the layers of the sadness that comes with this day. I will wear a yellow flower pin made by a friend to honor my darling babe. It will be bittersweet.

But in the rawness, I will pray for grace to get through it. I will remind myself that it is an incredible blessing to be a mother - whether to a child on this earth or in heaven. I am forever grateful for the gift we were given. So on this day I say: blessings to all you mothers, and blessings to all you who long to be mothers. My heart lies somewhere in between.

Part of me hates these words. Hates how razor-sharp solitude infiltrates them, cuts them from the inside out. I hear her heart, the hollow thud of the in-between, like the sound of a shovel hitting a coffin, like emptiness where there should be fullness. We still knew hurt, still wept, still longed for our daughter while we were contemplating this gigantic shift in our lives. It would seem, then, that the good thing to do is about-face, slip noiselessly back into the known and make sure that the uneasiness and unbalancing effect of our grief is segregated, neutralized. No big changes. No big moves. No big sacrifices. To upset our routine was a dangerous proposition. If we could just ensure that every other area in our life is normal, is predictable, is stable, it would allow us to heal sooner. That will be a good thing.

The Greater: Allowing grief to produce big changes.

If there's one thing you believe after your world is flipped over, it's that you deserve to lie down in the fetal position until someone or something else turns it right side up. It seems necessary, even wise. Books on grief, however creepy their covers may be, agree on this point. "Try not to make any big life changes in the first year after the tragedy" is the general consensus. We were at eight months, evidently four months away from claiming sound minds. This theory showed itself in the furrowed brows of friends, family, and strangers when we mentioned moving; that smile that's intended to communicate "I'm supportive" which in fact says, "Oh no, we've lost them." But we'd been found - God had made himself known to us at such an intimate level in the eight months after losing Emma; our hearts were in tune with his will, and we knew that a new path was right. A new path was exciting. A new path meant losing our life to gain it, losing our comfort to gain our calling, losing our past to gain our future, losing our mourning to gain our gladness, losing the dejection of an empty nursery for the hope of a full one. How could we avoid this? How could we not be absolutely thrilled, captivated, and committed to this newness?

The Good: Financial stability.

It is good to be employed in the midst of a recession. It is good to stay at a job that you've enjoyed, that you've found purpose in, that pays you money. It is good to know exactly where that money is coming from and when you'll get it. It is good because in a life that had become increasingly out of control, a reliable job offered me a more solidified illusion that I was in control. More of a provider for Julia. A better steward of God-given resources. To be a husband with a job, with a plan, with an irrefutable explanation for how things are going to "work out", is a very good thing.

The Greater: Reliance on Christ for stability.

Having a job does not mean you are relying on yourself rather than God, of course. And I would certainly have to look for a part-time job as soon as we moved to Ventura. But for Julia and I, this potential move was about so much more than where I make money. It was a deliberate choice that was not about positioning ourselves closer to provisions, but closer to the Provider. Not closer to gifts, but closer to the Giver. But make no mistake, this is most definitely a choice; and not a natural one. I am convinced that of all the illusions we live with and live for, control is the most attractive and most accepted. Of course we deny this with 'Christian' mottoes slapped on coffee mugs, sayings we toss out like the contents of a junk drawer: "We are not in control. God is in control." But look closer, and should you judge by actions instead of careless words, you would no doubt discover that we pine for control like addicts lusting for a fix. We ignore that we can do absolutely nothing to ensure the safety of those we love. We ignore that we are so painfully finite that we cannot even see a millisecond into the future. We ignore that we could die today and stand before God. And so often, our churches and our families and our friends do nothing to expose this illusion - instead, we are all content to exist as people fully accustomed to lying about how aggressively and how completely we strive for control of our own lives. Ultimately, we are so accustomed that we lose the ability to feel even slightly convicted that our selfish grabs for God's rightful role has rendered Jesus the illusion and our counterfeit control the accepted reality. As addicts, we do not listen to that still voice in the quiet that says, "Aren't you exhausted? Aren't you so very tired?" Because for us, money equals control, and control is king - so we secretly accumulate, careful to appear dependent on Christ, yet demanding that our finances free us from fears; taking solace in our budgets over our Bibles, our savings plan over our Creator's plan, our wallets over our God. But do you ever picture it, your meeting with God after death? Do you ever feel, momentarily, a twinge of dread at the thought of his questions: Why, when you knew of my power and promises, my everlasting grace and love for you, did you settle for such a pitiful, isolating existence?

Why did you choose the slavery of your own control over the freedom of faith in me alone? And what could you say to him in return? Wouldn't the deceptions and justifications and rationalizations you carried through your life of safety and ease evaporate into thin air? Wouldn't all those years of worrying and projecting and preparing for possible disappointment feel utterly wasted? Wouldn't you suddenly be overwhelmed by all the fullness that could have been had you simply stopped straining for control and lived as though Christ were actually real? How sad and how haunting a scene to imagine - you, a child of God, finally acknowledging the worth and glory of your heavenly Father, begging like a condemned man for a second chance to abandon the trappings of the finite world to truly follow him.

Julia and I would no longer buy into the illusion of control. We had found peace in relying on Christ in the midst of our suffering precisely because we experienced his presence so tangibly. We had lost everything, and yet we had gained Jesus. So decisions that would not lead to experiencing and displaying his love more completely seemed empty, temporary, and unnecessary. We were supremely confident that relying on God in the midst of financial uncertainties would draw us nearer still to our Maker – a result worth pursuing. As I thought ahead about investing in our new church, and as I talked with the director of the homeless ministry, my heart beat with more force, in tandem with the pulse of my soul. I knew the joy of relying on Christ far outweighs persistent fears about money, stability, or discomfort - this joy came from choosing the greater.

The Good: Amazing community.

This is the good that cost me sleep while deliberating over the move. This is the good that distracted and redirected my prayers, made me almost deaf to the will of the Lord, the good that says you never have to say goodbye for God. This is because the community we had in Pasadena was far beyond good. It was phenomenal. I worked and shared life with some of the most thoughtful, loving, challenging, and inspiring people in the world. This is biased, yes, but not inaccurate. I taught with them, I learned with them, I hiked mountains in Peru with them, Julia and I shared meals and laughs and memories with them, and we saw Christ's love and comfort displayed through them in our darkest hours. My affection and respect for each and every one of them cannot be overstated - I counted myself beyond blessed every time we shared a beer, a brat, a game of basketball, a thoughtful discussion, a vision of the future together. To see these dear brothers and sisters everyday, to know the next gathering is just around the corner, to rely on their strength and selflessness; these are all good things.

The prospect of moving away from this community carried with it a deep-seated sadness. It messed with my mind, because it never makes sense that we should ever have to leave our families or friends. Sure, leave our financial stability and comfort, leave our self-made plans, leave our wicked ways behind, but we should never need to leave those we love and lean on. To ensure we have their support, to see our calls to serve Christ on this planet through the lens of family attachment, through the perspective of friendship retention, seems like a very wise thing, a very good thing.

The Greater: Christ above all community.

I have always been fascinated by the following exchanges in Luke, chapter nine:

59 (Jesus) said to another man, "Follow me." But he
replied, "Lord, first let me go and bury my father."
60 Jesus said to him, "Let the dead bury their own dead,
but you go and proclaim the kingdom of God."
61 Still another said, "I will follow you, Lord; but first let
me go back and say goodbye to my family."
62 Jesus replied, "No one who puts a hand to the plow
and looks back is fit for service in the kingdom of God."

Two men with two different proclamations of good. The first desires to honor his father with a proper, culturally expected burial; the second is genuinely concerned with returning to his family, with ensuring bonds are not broken, that bridges between them are not burned. Then Jesus answers with one proclamation of the greater - do not turn back from the task you have been given; go and make disciples where I have called you. The part that irks me here is that Jesus deems the two proclamations mutually exclusive. In other words, Jesus seems to say that if you look back, if you hold on to your family and friends, you are not fit to be his disciple. I want this to be inaccurate. I want a plump professor with a PhD to soften this blow with a careful justification. The call of Christ requires rejection, yes. But of sin, of possessions, of positions, of worldliness, but not people we love. That seems ridiculous, even impossible. Perhaps what upsets me most is thinking about these men. The first: Does he have a mother? Is she bowed down to the dirt, weeping beside her dead husband? Is she gasping, scared to death, lonely and desperate, hands shuddering as she waits for her son to pick her up, carry her home, whisper in her ear that everything will be okay; that he will take care of it all, that he will give this man who raised him from infancy the burial he deserves? Is Jesus honestly telling him to let the dead bury their own dead? What of grace, what of understanding? Surely our Lord and Savior would not expect that we depart from our families so abruptly and so definitively, especially in a time of need, as though they have no more value than the dry dust of a decayed body. The second man: What damage will be done by leaving without a goodbye? Have his parents sacrificed everything for him, has his father worked day and night to provide a future for him, and are there now expectations for him to follow their advice, pick the path they suggest, remain close because that's what their family has always done? Would this man's family not see him as reckless and unfeeling, throwing away the ties they assume God has ordained to remain connected? Is Jesus actually saying that to think of family, to act on behalf of them, to prioritize them, is really akin to looking back as you push the plow, akin to furrowing a crooked row of crops, and therefore disqualifying you as a true disciple? Perhaps this bothers me when I place myself as the third man: I am at the foot of Jesus - "I will follow you, Lord, but please let me go and hold my daughter; let me say goodbye." And he says to me, "Let the dead bury their own dead, but you go and proclaim the kingdom of God." This seems cold, indifferent.

But at the heart of this is a return to the essential question from Christ: Do you love me most? If the answer is yes, then family, even my one and only daughter, is always secondary. Jesus says in Matthew 11:37-39, "If you love your father or mother more than you love me, you are not worthy of being mine; or if you love your son or daughter more than me, you are not worthy of being mine. If you refuse to take up your cross and follow me, you are not worthy of being mine. If you cling to your life, you will lose it; but if you give up your life for me, you will find it." And so I know that elevating people I love equal to or over the treasure of Jesus Christ is idolatry, is sowing a forked path, is pursuing a slow death over a filled life. Does this feel true? Yes. But does it feel normative? No. Maybe this is because I have rarely if ever heard a pastor passionately commit to illuminating the implications of these texts. Perhaps because in most of the churches I've attended, the unspoken agreement amongst the leaders and the congregation is that family can be equal to God, that the phrase, "I need to do what's best for my family" MUST be hung on the wall next to "take up your cross and follow me." Perhaps, if I'm brutally honest, it doesn't feel normal to me because I am aware that deep down, I am desperately afraid that if I leave the serenity and safety of my family and friends, God will not actually show up or satisfy me. Then I am aware once again that my faith is shriveled, that my god is my people, and my measure of joy and happiness is ultimately determined by the health, safety, and availability of individuals I expect to fulfill me the way only God can.

Such were the thoughts writhing inside me as I weighed the possibility of leaving this community. But the fresh waters of repentance wash over; I am realigned. I re-grip the plow and look forward at the bountiful harvest set before me in Christ. In Christ alone.

It reminds me of this poem I love so much:

"Obedience" by George MacDonald

I said: "Let me walk in the fields."
He said: "No, walk in the town."
I said: "There are no flowers there."
He said: "No flowers, but a crown."

I said: "But the skies are black;
There is nothing but noise and din."
And He wept as He sent me back -
"There is more," He said; "there is sin."

I said: "But the air is thick,
And fogs are veiling the sun."
He answered: "Yet souls are sick,
And souls in the dark undone!"

I said: "I shall miss the light,
And friends will miss me, they say."
He answered: "Choose tonight
If I am to miss you or they."

I pleaded for time to be given.
He said: "Is it hard to decide?
It will not seem so hard in heaven
To have followed the steps of your Guide."

I cast one look at the fields,
Then set my face to the town;
He said, "My child, do you yield?
Will you leave the flowers for the crown?"

Then into His hand went mine;
And into my heart came He;
And I walk in a light divine,
The path I had feared to see.

Yes, we would have to say goodbye to these wonderful people, but not without hope. For besides the anticipation of more Jesus, we knew our community would grow - that we would come to know and love and serve alongside brothers and sisters at Reality, that we would be blessed by kinship with the hurting and vulnerable in the city of Ventura. This we knew was the greater path.

None of these choices were easy, and the questions and concerns continually raged on. But ultimately, we chose what was revealed as the greater path - moving to Ventura. I remember being strengthened by this assertion from David Platt, who, in his book *Radical Together*, both challenges and affirms us with his perspective on the good versus greater: "I propose that we must put everything on the table. We have to put everything, even good things...up for reconsideration before God, releasing them wholly to him and asking him to show us his priorities and purposes for each...we must be willing to sacrifice good things...in order to experience the great things of God."[9]

[9] Platt, David. *Radical Together*. Multnomah Books. 2011.

CHAPTER TWELVE

- SHARING -

"...contact makes us so grateful we want to cry and dance and cry and cry. In a moment of clarity, you finally understand why boxers, who want so badly to hurt each other, can rest their heads on the shoulders of their opponents, can lean against one another like tired lovers, so thankful for a moment of peace."

- Dave Eggers, from 'The Accident'

A miraculous blessing occurred a month or so after we moved. I had been looking for a job. My desire was to find a position that was part-time or incredibly flexible so that I could still give a substantial part of my week to the homeless ministry. I understood that the odds were against me: Bad Economy + Choosy Job Seeker = Sorry you married me, Julia. But out of nowhere, a craigslist posting caught my eye, and it wasn't the "$40,000 to be a surrogate mother!" or "You are the future of sales!" one;

it was a part-time instructor position for a small private academy only a block away from our new place. It was the perfect amount of hours and I had just the right credentials - it was like God had written the post himself. I applied, and two days later, I was set for an interview. It went remarkably well. Except for one crucial problem. I found out the teaching schedule would be everyday for literally the exact same hours the outreach runs its ministry. I dragged out of the interview feeling, as I have so many times over the past few years, conflicted and confused as to what God could possibly be doing. Why even direct me to what seemed to be the perfect job, let the hope bubble inside me, only to kick out the foundation and leave me with more questions than I had before I found it? I wanted so badly for it to work. This was the only interview I had gotten since I left Pasadena. Only the second person to even respond to one of my job inquiries. How could I turn it down? How could I knowingly perpetuate a rising dread that I would never find a job, that this whole moving to Ventura in faith thing was in fact foolish? Wasn't it just plain selfish to decline the offer? Didn't I have to be a responsible husband now? I prayed with Julia. Prayed with others. Prayed alone. And yet I already knew the answer. I knew it when they told me the conflicting times. For in my soul I knew that to move here specifically to serve this community, only to then avoid the actual context where that service would take place, was unthinkable. Julia saw it on my face, felt it in her own heart as well, and it was she who ultimately said I would need to turn it down; that God does not call us to serve those we are unwilling or unable to really know. So I talked with the head of school and told her about my passion for the ministry. I told her I really liked what I saw in their school, but that my heart was committed elsewhere. And then strange things started to happen. She wasn't angry. She didn't say, "Okay, have a nice day" and hang up either. She listened. Then responded in a way I never expected. She explained with a quivering voice that her brother had been homeless for 18 years, addicted to drugs, and had finally gotten clean two years ago. She stated that not enough people care about the homeless. That she commends what the outreach is doing. And later, to my ultimate surprise, that she would be willing to completely alter my teaching schedule so that I could continue my work at the ministry.

So between my questioning and lack of trust, God was already orchestrating what would be the best possible work situation for me. I was so humbled by the grace and power of our God. To step out in faith, and then see God answer so completely the longings of my heart brought such a potent thrill, and I was reminded that our God is big; so big. That as we give more and more of our control away to Christ, as we relinquish our need for comfort or safety or insulation from the what-if's, God is free to work wonders, faithful to set forth the greatest path for each of us, and overflowing with a grace that gives us more of him so that we might love like him. This crazy provision brings me back to a conversation I had with my dad about whether or not we should move to Ventura. I was so worried about not having a job, not having a place to live, not knowing how I would financially support my wife. He told me, very calmly and very lovingly, something I will never forget. He said, "Dan, it is easy for God to change small circumstances - jobs and places to live. It is much harder for God to change the heart of a man. But with a changed heart, he can do things beyond your comprehension."

~

We fell further in love with Ventura. Everywhere we looked it felt as though God was affirming our step of faith to move there. Our community at Reality grew. Our boldness in sharing our testimony with them grew with it. Their care and concern and willingness to share their own stories further confirmed that God was with us, working in us, and working through us. For me, spending such significant time at the homeless ministry was life-giving - my soul felt alive when I was there. The Holy Spirit is so active and Christ's handiwork so evident among this community of hurting individuals whom God cherishes so abundantly. To offer love in any capacity to people that are so often downcast to the point of hopelessness by their labels: "homeless", "addict", or "crazy", was to encounter Christ in a new and heartrending way. There, standing in the courtyard before serving a meal, it was continually confirmed to me that humanity's aches sting the same at their root, and though we had completely different histories, I could sit side by side with the fifty year old man who had just lost his home, the drug addict trying to quit but shivering from withdrawals, the mother-to-be scared to death of her baby being born at the river bottom, the schizophrenic warning of the coming Apocalypse, and offer all the same words of support I had previously received during grief, with the same effect: comfort and hope.

In all spheres of our new life in Ventura, God allowed our hearts to run head first into the hearts of others. There was Rita, a 55 year old woman who had come to the outreach because she had been fired from her job a year before, kicked out of her apartment, and had run out of friends' couches to crash on, scared to death of spending another night on the streets. She was vulnerable, sweet, ingratiating; like a grandmother you wish you could somehow take back to your childhood. Miraculously, the day after we prayed for her, she was hired at a local restaurant - she had been looking without success for eleven months. She accepted Jesus Christ that Sunday. Weeks later, however, I passed by her in the courtyard and noticed she was weeping. I sat down and asked what happened. She still had the job, and she was supposed to move into a new apartment with her son. Why was she crying? It is simple - because it could all crumble to pieces again. She was replaying those nights in the park, the numbing cold and hollow dog barks and haunting cackle of lurking thieves; and the anxiety was boiling over. This I understood completely. Because even after you've been lifted from the pit, it's impossible not to worry about falling into the next one. Will it be deeper? So I told Rita our story, my similar concerns. I showed her the verses I hold onto from Philippians 4 - "Do not be anxious about anything, but in everything by prayer and supplication with thanksgiving let your requests be made known to God. And the peace of God, which surpasses all understanding, will guard your hearts and your minds in Christ Jesus." I shared that for me, the critical phrase is 'with thanksgiving', that despite my anxieties about repeat tragedies, I try to start my prayers with a thankful heart. A list of all that I am grateful for, all the minute details of everything extraordinary God has done in my life since losing my daughter. This corrects my view of God; he is seen as he should be - a provider that is above all circumstances. Yes, Rita was still crying, but now in remembrance of God's faithfulness, not in angst of his forgetfulness. So we prayed and hugged each other and I tossed out a stupid joke that made her giggle.

I knew of Sean because he was in our community group at Reality. Last year, his wife of 30 years lost her battle with cancer. The physical descent was far too unexpected and far too quick. She was an incredible woman; the type of person who confirms the existence of the Holy Spirit because it permeates so fiercely from her every word and deed. In the wake of her death, Sean was devastated, confused, grasping for the comfort only God can bring. But I have never met a man with faith like him.

Faith so broad, so pure, so evident. Faith that allowed him to praise God with the fervor of Job and the precision of Paul. I walked up to him one Sunday, and though I knew he was still grieving, I asked him if he would consider being a mentor to me. I knew it was presumptuous to request counsel from a man who was hurting so badly, but I also know that despair thirsts for purpose, because purpose is what you desperately hope can remain after desolation. We started meeting weekly for coffee. For those two hours each week, time stood still. We would tell tales to one another; fond memories of his wife and their love together, of Julia and Emma, and of God's grace. But more importantly, it was a space to lament, to mourn, to encourage each other, to pray that strength and courage would seep into us once more. To be honest, I don't know whom was mentoring whom, and it didn't remotely matter, because authentic, de-masked fellowship never elevates a person, it only and always elevates the God who is powerful enough to shine his light as a bridge between two dark cities that would, to the weakened eye, appear miles apart.

There is Marion, our 97 year old next-door neighbor. She is a widow and a warrior. Her husband, who fought in both World War I and World War II, died almost 20 years ago. She lives on her own and spends most of her time painting, but also loves bingo, getting her hair permed, watching dysfunctional court shows on TV, and scaring the crap out of our other neighbors when she pulls into the communal driveway at 55 miles per hour.

She is feisty and firm, but soft as a peach inside. We love her. A few months ago, she went to the emergency room because she wasn't feeling well and her leg hurt. Apparently along the way she had a heart-attack that she didn't even notice. Julia and I brought flowers. She talked our ears off, and perhaps because she was lying in a hospital bed, she began a narrative of her very full life. Triumphs and catastrophes and a love story that Cary Grant and Ingrid Bergman should have been cast in. Careers and wars and friends that have long since passed away. However, there was one thing absent from the story - children. We discovered that Marion had not a single family member who was packing up, buying airline tickets, and flying to see her. No grown son driving across town to hold her hand, to tell her, "Don't worry, Mom. We're right here." And what I hated most was what I saw on her face when we waved goodbye that first time: fear. Julia demanded that we visit her everyday that she was at the hospital. And so we did, for the whole month she was admitted. We brought her the paper, of which she only read an obscure section called "Dotty's Thoughts" or something like that; we brought cookies and banana bread and drawings from our niece. Then we would pray for her. For painless sleep and for healing. I would have to lean in close because she's half-deaf, but I remember thinking this is how I should pray with people anyway; bursting through even the physical barriers to share a communion with Christ. She would laugh so hard, sometimes toothless if we caught her at a sans-dentures moment. When Marion finally came back home, she was beyond thrilled. She shook her head, waving her finger at Julia and I, shouting, "You people! I've never met people like you before!"

There's Joseph whom I talked with often as he tried to escape the snares of the river bottom. A woman in our community group who until we shared our story, did not feel freedom to grieve the unborn child that had died a year before. A woman several states away who read Julia's blog, mourning the two year anniversary of her husband's death when Julia's brave honesty and fearless faith in Christ gave her the strength to press on, to keep fighting. And there are so many more stories, so many more amazing encounters.

This is not to our credit, not even close. This is God's perfect design and the devil's perpetual fear, that we might realize just how important we are to one another. Emma's death roused this sleeping necessity inside Julia and I. The subtle disguises we had always draped ourselves in, remote and impervious to others, had shed like snake-skin, cast-off amid the aftermath. We had no back-up facade on stand-by; we sewed no replacement cloak. We were on display, susceptible. And it was partnered with an offensive sensation - hearts throbbing more violently, more loosely because our chest cavities weren't caved in from the armor of our false fronts anymore. But this repellent feeling converted to invigoration with each new person's willingness to love us despite the off-putting exposure of our naked humanity. To be loved behind the masks we wear, this endorses the uncaged heart, which gives birth to the transformed heart. And the transformed heart is blind to all costumes in the bustling masquerade around us - it sees only fellow human beings, equal friends, and pines for the salvation of their souls.

CHAPTER THIRTEEN

- RESTORING -

"Blessed are the hearts that can bend; they shall never be broken."

- Albert Camus

The desert always calls back. Always beckons us to return and lie down. The one-year anniversary of Emma's death was approaching. This seems true: women who lose their children like Julia did get pregnant soon after, and that seems fair. This was true: Julia wasn't getting pregnant, and that did not seem fair. Many long nights in late 2010, as we reached for optimism like toddlers grabbing at dandelion fragments on a windy day, Julia and I whispered fragile visions to each other - one being that we would have another baby in 2011. We would lie there, audibly imagining the looks on our families' faces, the happiness lining our friends' smiles, the mini parade promenading through her maternity unit as our new child was born bellowing a cry of life - redemption would reign. But it was August, 2011. No such visions unfolding. How could we have avoided the expectation that waiting was behind us? How could we fathom that after all of these dreams had withered, there were now more dreams to cast off as rotting carcasses on the starving road we thought God would deliver us from? Wouldn't a new child bring God more glory, more fame? Job lost his family. He wrestled and questioned and finally understood and gave glory to God who was his whole portion. But then he got a new family. I liked that model; I wanted that model. Not as a replacement for Emma, not as an expected payment for loyalty or obedience, but because my faith tells me God is a Father who delights in giving good gifts to his children. Once again we were confronted with his ways hovering far above ours. His sovereignty combating our ever-confused "why?" We were confronted with the lie that perhaps this is our only lot in life, our only calling; to be that couple created by God to be the creators of new dreams that never come true.

And the desert calls back. And it seems a lonely siren song composed only for us. What does it mean for Julia to be a mother without her child? It means a grocery store is not a grocery store - it is suffocating procession of women whom she is, and whom she is not. The young woman newly married picking out frozen peas: I am you because all who see our flat stomachs and empty carts assume we are not mothers, but you are not me because I have been a mother to a beautiful little girl. The woman pregnant with her first child, bearing back aches as she retrieves a carton of milk: I am you because I too have had life squirm inside my womb and felt first kicks and stretches that speak to a unique personality already forming, and I too rested my palm on my bulging stomach as if to say "shhh, mommy's here"; but you are not me because your baby is healthy, is growing rightly, will be delivered alive and will squirm and smile beside you on a high chair this Christmas. The woman carrying her new baby girl on a front pack while two toddlers race between her legs: I am you because I love my daughter as you do, I held my daughter in the hospital as you did, I marked and measured and traced our shared facial features, and I knew her then as intimately as a mother ever can; but you are not me because your daughter was allowed to look back at you, could know you as her mother in this world, and you are wearing your evidence of motherhood like radiant garments for all to see, and you are included in the club of legitimate mothers who are invited to discuss parenting and play dates while I, with my empty arms and empty womb, have little to offer in this the realm I've always wanted to exist in. Another woman, eyes weathered by a past ordeal, holding her one child more tightly than the others: I am you because we have both lost children, we have both suffered through it, and we both desperately miss our little ones; but you are not me because you conceived again, you are holding pink and pudgy atonement in your arms, you are cradling broken dreams glued back together, while I am wondering if I should throw the fractured pieces of mine into the ocean.

I judge once more that our waiting feels Biblical. Thousand-year waiting. Israel-style waiting. And I lift my eyes to God and my cards flop face-up on the table: The noose is tightening and You are departing again. My wife, whose heart has been mangled, needs but one soothing ointment, one rehabilitating reclamation, and that is life growing inside her once more. Why do you withhold? Have we not been faithful? Have we not been steadfast in our love to you? Have we not given you all the glory? I hear his promise from Psalm 126 - "Those who sow in tears shall reap with shouts of joy!" No, I say, they do not. We who sow in tears just move over and plow the next row. We watch everyone else sit back and enjoy the beauty of their own personal harvest while our backs break and sobs suffuse from worn ducts you do not dare dry up. I yell back Lamentations 3 - "You have made me chew on gravel. You have rolled me in the dust. Peace has been stripped away, and I have forgotten what prosperity is...'My splendor is gone! Everything I had hoped for from the Lord is lost!' The thought of my suffering...is bitter beyond words. I will never forget this awful time, as I grieve over my loss." And he speaks Hebrews 10 softly to me, each word infinitely calm, infinitely patient - "Do not throw away your confidence, which has a great reward...We are not of those who shrink back and are destroyed, but of those who have faith and preserve their souls." I do not want to hear this, though. I want to challenge it like a foolish child. 'What is faith, really?' I say. He answers with Hebrews 11 - "What is faith? It is the constant assurance that what we hope for is going to happen. It is the evidence of things we cannot yet see." I know this cerebrally. But I want to believe it in my soul. I want a reminder of this constant assurance. Psalm 145 rushes in - "The Lord is faithful in all his words and kind in all his works. The Lord upholds all who are falling and raises up all who are bowed down. The eyes of all look to Him, and He gives them their food in due season. He opens His hand; He satisfies the desire of every living thing. The Lord is righteous in all his ways and kind in all his works. The Lord is near to all who call on him, to all who call on him in truth. He fulfills the desire of those who fear him; he also hears their cry and saves them." Yes, I do really know this. I remember this. I remember God's exceeding goodness to us, his exceeding comfort for us, the joy he has produced in us through revealing the supreme value of Jesus Christ, and the plan that is surely for our good and his glory. So I repent, but not without another plea from Psalm 119 - "Remember your word to your servant, in which you have made me hope. This is my comfort in my affliction, that your promise gives me life." His forgiveness showers over me and the treasure of God himself rises above all earthly desires, including a new child. But this does not mean I forget the dream of more children, but simply that I step into the rays of light effusing from the truths of his character and I am strengthened. I make the turn and announce Jeremiah's passionate proclamation, "Yet I still dare to hope when I remember this: The faithful love of the Lord never ends! His mercies never cease. Great is his faithfulness; his mercies begin afresh each morning. I say to myself, "The Lord is my inheritance; therefore, I will hope in him!"

And yet the desert calls back. But we choose not to answer, we will not even turn our shoulders. For we are not of those who shrink back. We are of those who dare to hope.

CHAPTER FOURTEEN

- REJOICING -

"You do not need to know precisely what is happening, or exactly where it is all going. What you need is to recognize the possibilities and challenges offered by the present moment, and to embrace them with courage, faith and hope."

- Thomas Merton

It is a windy Saturday afternoon and I am leaning on a picnic table in a Ventura park steps from the Pacific. Balloons and paper lanterns and bright flowers abound. I am gazing out at a sea of family and friends who stare back, waiting for me to speak. But before I do, I take it in. I let what I'm seeing synthesize with what I've been processing all day. One year ago, our daughter Emma Jo snuck silently from this world into eternal glory. One year ago, her death dyed the parchment of our lives like charcoal etched in fury on a white page. One year ago, God seemed silent. But now, gathered before me, nothing but the loudest harmony of togetherness, the loudest vibrations of love. What do I say? How can I possibly articulate what I feel after 365 days of falling and stumbling and walking with my God through misery, petition, and praise? I can't. It is impossible. Of course that hasn't stopped me before. So I step up, clear my throat, plant my feet atop the table, and start to speak.

~

Several months prior, Julia was doing some reading online when she discovered a woman named Sarah Erwin. Sarah's son, Holden, was born on a Saturday; August 28, 2010, three days before Emma died. Holden weighed 7 lbs., 5 oz. He was a big boy. A handsome boy. But he too was born into heaven. He, like Emma, first opened his eyes to see Jesus' face instead of his mother's. He too left parents pulled to pieces. And like us, Sarah and her husband were, despite the wreckage, confronted with God's kindness and comfort, his grace and mercy, and the joyous reality of their son's ultimate peace in a paradise they could not possibly imagine.

God was working through them in miraculous ways, namely through a non-profit they established called Holden Uganda. Its mission is to "spread the love of Christ with people...by providing clean drinking water, through Artesian wells, to African communities. Between

500 and 2000 Ugandan people are given hope through clean drinking water with each well. Also, each well is dedicated to a baby or child who went to heaven before his/her parents." Julia knew the minute she read this that Holden Uganda was the foundation we were to partner with for a celebration to honor the life of our daughter. We knew from our past research and interactions with Africa that the lack of clean water was a significant factor in the crippling malnutrition, dehydration, and disease that plagues certain areas of the continent, specifically in Uganda, specifically in rural areas where water is often scarce. We knew there were infants and children with no other choice but to ingest dirty water, daring death with each gulp. We knew their mothers and fathers wanted nothing more than to care for them, to protect them. We loved that Holden Uganda not only provided clean water, but also stimulated the local economy by employing only Ugandans to build, oversee, and sustain the wells. We also knew that we wanted to host a special gathering for Emma's one year birthday, something that would remind everyone of what a wonderful gift she was to us all. A time and space to remember God's faithfulness in granting us the blessing of eight months with our daughter, and his faithfulness in granting us strength to endure the last twelve months without her. So the connection with Sarah was made, the party was planned, invitations sent out, and as it neared, the excitement magnified and multiplied.

~

As I look out at this crowd, I see a hundred people who prayed for us. I see a hundred people who wept with us. I see a hundred people who hoped beyond circumstances with us. Many of them do not know one another. They are here from all over, from different places and phases in our journey, but they share the common bond of loving us and our daughter dearly. In each pair of eyes I see a specific sacrifice, a specific feat of selflessness. My friend who was there when I got the call - he alone carries that horrific memory, he alone put the first hand on my shoulder as I wailed. Julia's mom - the one who lived with us for weeks after, the one who never stopped nurturing and cooking and caring, the one who strapped herself in the burning chair beside us. Her dad - who mourned with wisdom, spoke with integrity, and shepherded us toward Christ. The couple that never stopped calling, never stopped praying, never stopped speaking words of consolation. The brand new mom and dad who cherish their child more completely because of Emma. My parents - encouragement personified, beacons of light to us as we navigated stormy seas. A new friend from our church - he loves us as if he's known us his whole life, loves our daughter as if she were his own. A group of friends who have traveled up from Pasadena - my reassurance that brotherhood and sisterhood in Christ is not a fiction but a fact that breeds jubilee. And on and on, each face smiling, each person still desiring above all to offer their love without stipulations.

I tell them thank you. I tell them that they have proven to Julia and I that Jesus Christ is real, that there is no more appropriate way to say it. I tell them that their love has sustained and strengthened us. That this party is also to honor them, for their courage in caring for two lonely, grief-stricken lepers that they could've easily kept their distance from. I tell them about Holden Uganda, about the significance of providing water to these communities, about the value of life-giving wells coming out of life-taking darkness and death. About this being a part of Emma's story of redemption. I tell them to remember - this is an occasion to celebrate, not to mourn. I tell them we gratefully proclaim that our daughter is in heaven, that she is immune to the maladies of this earth. We proclaim that God rescues, God comforts, and God redeems. We proclaim that always and forever, God raises beauty out of ashes. Lastly, I read this poem:

Emma Jo

We imagine that you walk in heaven,
that Jesus is beside you.
We imagine that your steps are feather light,
that you are robed in sweetest joy.

We imagine that you worship with the angels,
that they call you by name.

We rejoice that you do not weep,
do not know fear, or shame, or sorrow.
We rejoice that you will never suffer,
that your body is unbroken and your soul complete.
We rejoice that your days are drenched in peace,
that your destiny is to dine with Christ.

We celebrate today that you have been so purely loved,
so adored and honored and cherished by so many,
We celebrate today that your life has not been defined by
brevity, but by the full gravity of God's faithfulness.
We celebrate today that death has been defeated,
Jesus reigns, and we shall hold you again.

~

There is a pleasant hum in my soul right now - it reverberates with the mellifluous pulse of this present fellowship. Fellowship that is a vanguard for what will be experienced in heaven. Men and women from different backgrounds and backdrops and hurts and healings, gathered over a warm meal with warm companionship saturated in one permeating truth: God is love. I offer a prayer of appreciation, that God saw fit to fashion this day with his presence, with a firm glimpse of His Kingdom come.

~

A month or two has passed; I am once again looking at a multitude of faces staring back at me. Picture after picture after picture sent to us from Sarah Erwin. There is a striking Ugandan woman in a floral dress with radiant eyes, her small child clasped on her shoulders like a backpack. She leans over, dipping a yellow container underneath a steady stream of pure water pouring from a sturdy spout. There is a group of five young men posing, one laughing, one smirking, one forcing his lips together so as to avoid busting up. One grins up at the camera, dropping his yellow canister to the water. These are images of a well in Emma Jo's honor. Well #35 for Holden Uganda. It is between Bulangira and Petete in Eastern Uganda. It will give clean water to over one thousand men, women, and children. Written on the well's cement face are Emma Jo's name, her birthday, and a verse - Isaiah 61:3 - "Provide for those who grieve in Zion – to bestow on them a crown of beauty instead of ashes, the oil of joy instead of mourning, and a garment of praise instead of a spirit of despair. They will be called oaks of righteousness, a planting of the LORD for the display of his splendor."

There are more pictures. In this one, the sun is blazing and you can almost feel the heat emanating from the photograph. A woman is by herself, dipping her hands into the cool stream of water, rubbing the dirt from her fingertips. Another woman gathers water while her young son crawls beside her. Then, a picture that brings tears - it is packed with children, all under 10, rallying around the well with Christmas-morning glee. They are shoulder to shoulder, smile to smile, all exuding immeasurable joy as the water flows freely from the pump. This is Emma Jo's second well, #36, called "kabiribiriti". The Ugandan doctor who leads the building teams wrote this, "Kabiribiriti well is located in an isolated environment and serves about 800 people. The community has wanted to make that water clean for a long time because they were sharing with cows. Their dream has finally come true and they are grateful to the donor that sponsored the well."

Still more images. Three beautiful little girls with bright dresses, gathering water. Then two mothers, one pregnant, arrived at the well, and as the container fills with water their eyes fill with the relief of a parent who gets to provide for their children. Then my personal favorite - nine little boys lined across the edge of the well, dancing. Yes, they are dancing and I want to join them. Below, their grandfather is cupping water between his palms and drawing it to his lips. This is Emma's third well, #37, between Butebo and Kakoro. It has been constructed as a double-pump well. It will serve over 3,000 people from four different villages who before this point did not have access to clean water. The scripture engraved is 1 Corinthians 13:3 - "If I give all I possess to the poor and give over my body to hardship that I may boast, but do not have love, I gain nothing."

Over $6,000 dollars raised. Three wells. 5,000 Ugandans now drinking crystal water drawn from cool depths beneath the soil of their own homeland. And Emma Jo, a little girl who never took a breath on this earth, a little girl who some could say came and left giving nothing, at the heart of this gift of life given and multiplied. Where man sees our ruin, God sees our ransom. Where man sees only dark corners, God sees a doorway. Where man sees everything breaking, God sees everything mending. And where man sees the premature death of a child, God sees the perfect timing to bring her home and raise those left behind to life. He takes the wastelands we walk through and uses them to weave legacies that will not spoil.

~

I am reminded that God wastes nothing. Julia and I grew up thousands of miles away from each other. But we ended up at the same college, in the same freshman English class, in the same row of desks. We got married and established the dream to have kids. But we ended up battling infertility, which led us to God's will not our own, which directed us toward adoption. We were led to Africa, where we assumed our first child would hail from. But we got pregnant with Emma, which postponed the adoption, which ignited the excitement for both dreams, which was a new future lavished with happiness. But we lost Emma, which seemed to kill all dreams, which made us believe everything was for nothing, which reduced us to ashes. But God raised beauty from those ashes through his comfort, which spoke breath into our lungs and hopes into our hearts, which led us by his infinite love, which carried us through the bottomless canyons of doubt and desperation. But God continued bolstering our belief in him, which led us to an eternal perspective, which led to an understanding that there was more to do on this planet, which led us to honoring our daughter, his creation, with a celebration that would ultimately bring life and liberation from suffering to thousands of men, women, and children half a globe away in the very place our hearts yearned to support years before: Africa. And what else? I don't know.

I can say what I envision: Eighty years from now, an old woman will lie on a bed in her home at the heart of a thriving Ugandan village, wrinkles running her riven face, decades of life and love and happiness behind her; she will place a crinkled hand that is rife with arthritis but abounding in solace atop the hands of her crying children and grandchildren, offer a wink and a grin that says she is without pain and without worry, then close her eyes, leave the earth, and enter glory. In heaven, she will run into the arms of Jesus. And singing and dancing and clapping beside him will be our daughter, Emma Jo. And this Ugandan woman will walk over to her, and these two bodies made whole will embrace. And the woman will whisper to Emma that when she was but a child, her whole family was on the verge of death. She watched as her brothers and sisters, scourged with horrific bouts of dehydration, wept for help. But one day a miracle came. It came in the form of a well. It spouted clean water. They drank from it. They lived from it. She wondered one day why it came. What the writing on its wall meant. She received her answer. And then and there she fell in love with Jesus Christ. This love she poured over her whole family, her whole village, for decades to come, so that soon and very soon, we all might join together in the vast banquet hall of heaven as one body making one joyful noise. Yes, I believe this is a legacy that will never spoil. This is God's love here and hereafter.

CHAPTER FIFTEEN

- REFLECTING -

"Turn around and believe that the good news that we are loved is better than we ever dared hope, and that to believe in that good news, to live out of it and toward it, to be in love with that good news, is of all glad things in this world the gladdest thing of all. Amen, and come Lord Jesus."

- Frederick Buechner

The last and most persistent lie that we've often felt inclined to believe is that in the end, suffering produces more bad than good. It exposes God as hideous, not lovely. It pulls us further away from Christ rather than gravitating us toward him. But as we look back at the past year, we know this is not true, not even close, and that we must quickly and consistently annul ourselves from this gross deception. For above it all, the truest thing I can possibly articulate is that suffering has made us more like

Christ. Suffering has discarded and dismantled and dismembered everything we assumed was as essential to our survival as lungs and heart and bones. And yet we stride forward, stronger, for suffering has given us the one and only essential: Jesus Christ. So we rejoice in this fact that no matter the cost, no matter the hardship, this present suffering only spurs monumental movement toward our essential source of life, generates a significant and urgent re-shaping that allows us to more closely shadow the Son of Man, to resemble Christ who saved us. Julia and I have only to recollect, and see this is true.

We are more like Christ in our relationships because of suffering. We love more rightly. We empathize more extensively. We offer grace more purely. We give and accept service more freely. We forgive more radically. We tell the truth more completely. We encourage with more confidence. We preach faith in Christ with more boldness. We forgive more unconditionally. All because we have suffered.

We are more like Christ in our mission because of suffering. We care less about money. We care less about stability. We care less about earthly comfort. We care less about other's opinions of us. We care less about power, prestige, or position. And we care more about spreading the gospel. We care more about embodying the gospel. We care more about Christ leading us into the homes of the hurting. We care more about making decisions in light of the eternal instead of the temporal. We care more about our lives demanding an explanation with an answer that starts and ends with Jesus Christ. All because we have suffered.

We are more like Christ in our submission to God because of suffering. We submit more to God's sovereignty. We submit more to his ways above ours. We submit to his plans, his purposes, his priorities. We submit to his declaration that all this brokenness will be redeemed. All because we have suffered.

And we are more like Christ in our hope because of suffering. We still hope big. We still hope broadly. We still hope for an obnoxious litter of kids. We still hope for adoption from Africa, from America, from wherever in the world there are children without parents. We still hope that we'll discover new and amazing ways to serve the least of these. We still hope that a harvest of blessing is coming. We still hope that our story will wrap around your story like a warm blanket, like a touch from the Almighty, like a strangely dangerous and strangely beautiful proposition to believe in something bigger than yourself.

What is our future? Unsettled in the most settling way. Life will have no guarantees because we surrender to the one guarantee: Jesus Christ. We will look ahead through the lens of continued obedience - we could stay in Ventura for the rest of our lives or leave it tomorrow; we could delight in a second pregnancy or choose joy as we fight a new battle with infertility; we could see new dreams come to pass or witness God once again dismantle and re-shape our visions for his glory and our good. All could be taken away, and yet all will be given in Christ. Thus, the canvas of our future is rescued from the vandalism of fear and anxiety and returned to its rightful owner, the supreme artist, the loving God we call Father; he who renders our broken hearts whole, right where we are.

~

We miss our daughter. God, do we miss her. And we are so very tired sometimes. Trying to figure out why we are here and why we are breaking and why we are loved by God and why He feels so far away and why we hurt each other and why we need each other and why hope is as necessary as oxygen and why it seems to be in short supply is so very exhausting. It appears there is no order, there is no heavenly architect, there is no plan to salvage this apparently forsaken planet. It appears as though that force inside you that thrashes and kicks and shouts out for a savior will be forever waiting for an answer that is not coming. But please, please know that if you are still screaming inside, it means that you are still alive inside. And there is One who answers. There is One who shall bring forth this final resolution:

"Then I saw a new heaven and a new earth, for the old heaven and the old earth had disappeared. And the sea was also gone. And I saw the holy city, the new Jerusalem, coming down from God out of heaven like a bride beautifully dressed for her husband. I heard a loud shout from the throne, saying, 'Look, God's home is now among his people! He will live with them, and they will be his people. God himself will be with them. He will wipe every tear from their eyes, and there will be no more death or sorrow or crying or pain. All these things are gone forever.' And the one sitting on the throne said, 'Look, I am making everything new!' And then he said to me, 'Write this down, for what I tell you is trustworthy and true.' And he also said, 'It is finished! I am the Alpha and the Omega – the Beginning and the End. To all who are thirsty I will give freely from the springs of the water of life. All who are victorious will inherit all these blessings, and I will be their God, and they will be my children.'"

~

I imagine we are little children at the end of an old neighborhood block. It's late Autumn and the shivers of December's arrival creep underneath our coats. We are watching brittle, lifeless leaves shedding from a giant tree - like ancient clay plates, they shatter into a thousand flakes beneath our boots. We wonder why trees must lose their luster and die, be stripped naked, all their bones displayed, all that covered and consoled them removed. Why must the leaves of this tree die, while others stay alive and green all year? This is not fair.

And we are small. We cannot make sense of it. We only know that we are so very sad - we think that each leaf must claw and clamor, failing to hug its arms around the branch from which it is detaching, must feel fear as it floats to the freezing ground. This once magnificent tree, like a mother bereft of her children, is left bare and unprotected and cold all winter. We cry through our fingers, and want to bury ourselves on the concrete with the rest of the leaves. We don't want to live in a world where leaves die and trees are threadbare.

But a voice whispers, "Turn and look." And we do. We turn and look down the street. Through the hazy scope of eyes welled with tears, we take in the rows and rows and rows of trees lining the street, each shedding their own leaves. We see them from a different angle. From a wider view. Tree branches run into and over and around one another. The leaves create the loveliest impressionist painting; manifold shades of red and orange and yellow and green swirling and melding and mixing as they fall together - a cyclonic rainbow of burning colors. The trees are peeled, raw, and shuddering, but not alone; not alone like that one tree we focused on moments ago. Now we see that all the trees are united - their branches touch, like they are holding hands, like they care for one another, like Winter has come but they are rooted here for each other until Spring. And it is dazzling, the way those perished leaves dance with one another. Dance because they delight in their destiny: chosen by God to display that death has been overcome by beauty, loneliness overcome by love, and despair overcome by hope.

We are so honored to be the parents of Emma - our cherished one, our great inspiration, our most precious gift from God. We are so very, very proud of her. Because she changed everything. Everything. And we dream of her face, bright like the morning sun, lighting up when she greets us in heaven. Emma Jo, the little girl who blossomed boldly then left this world behind, has shown us that Death has no hold on those who truly know Life. Life where the neighboring branches intersect with ours, where we see the immaculate collage of death and re-birth through the eyes of the Creator, where all that has been lost is found in Him. And for this we are grateful, for this we choose to live.

- About the Author -

Daniel Walser grew up in Chicago and moved to California for college where he eventually met and married his wife, Julia. The Walsers are proud parents of Emma Jo, now in heaven, but whose memory has reached far and wide. Dan worked as a high school English teacher before beginning his current work in the non-profit sector.

For more on the Walsers' story, please visit:
www.tomakealife.com

Made in the USA
Charleston, SC
02 September 2012